# MONTANA BATTLEFIELDS

*1806–1877*

---

## NATIVE AMERICANS AND THE U.S. ARMY AT WAR

BY BARBARA FIFER

FARCOUNTRY
PRESS

ISBN 13: 978-1-56037-309-4
ISBN 10: 1-56037-309-1

©2005 Farcountry Press
Text ©2005 Barbara Fifer

Cover photo: Two Moon, 1878. Photograph by S. J. Morrow. COURTESY MONTANA HISTORICAL SOCIETY.
          Gattling gun battery, Fort Lincoln, D.T. 1877. Photograph by
          F. Jay Haynes. HAYNES FOUNDATION COLLECTION, MONTANA HISTORICAL SOCIETY.
Back cover photo: Curley, Crow scout. Date unknown. Photograph by O. S. Goff.
          COURTESY MONTANA HISTORICAL SOCIETY.

For more information on our books, write Farcountry Press,
P.O. Box 5630, Helena, MT 59604; call (800) 821-3874;
or visit www.farcountrypress.com.

Created, produced, and designed in the United States.
Printed in Canada.

09  08  07  06  05      1  2  3  4  5


Library of Congress Cataloging-in-Publication Data

Fifer, Barbara.
    Montana battlefields, 1806-1877 : Native Americans and the U.S. Army
at war / by Barbara Fifer.
       p. cm.
    Includes bibliographical references and index.
    ISBN 1-56037-309-1
1. Indians of North America--Montana--Wars. 2. Indians of North America--
Government policy--Montana. 3. Indians of North America--Montana--History--
19th century. 4. United States--Politics and government. 5. United States--History--
19th century. 6. United States--Race relations. I. Title.
    E78.M9F54 2005
    973.04'970786--dc22
                                                              2005013402

*For Mrs. G (Dort Getrost) of the summer adventures,*
*vast tolerance, and wicked sense of humor,*
*and Señor (Shearl Edler), the best schoolteacher of them all*

## Acknowledgments

Kermit Edmonds's kind generosity with his vast knowledge of frontier army history makes me wish that "thank you" had a superlative form that could come close to expressing my gratitude to him. Many thanks also to Shawn White Wolf for his consideration in vetting the manuscript, to Jessica Solberg for her enthusiastic and patient editing, and to Ann Seifert for her editing skills.

*B.F.*

# Table of Contents

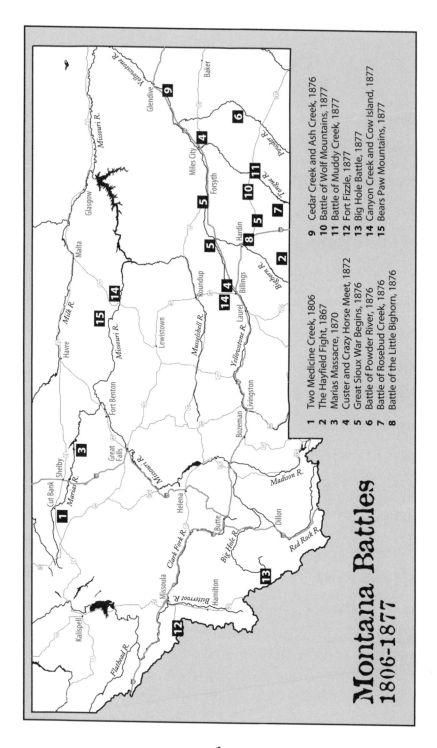

# Montana Battles 1806-1877

1  Two Medicine Creek, 1806
2  The Hayfield Fight, 1867
3  Marias Massacre, 1870
4  Custer and Crazy Horse Meet, 1872
5  Great Sioux War Begins, 1876
6  Battle of Powder River, 1876
7  Battle of Rosebud Creek, 1876
8  Battle of the Little Bighorn, 1876
9  Cedar Creek and Ash Creek, 1876
10  Battle of Wolf Mountains, 1877
11  Battle of Muddy Creek, 1877
12  Fort Fizzle, 1877
13  Big Hole Battle, 1877
14  Canyon Creek and Cow Island, 1877
15  Bears Paw Mountains, 1877

# INTRODUCTION

For many states of the United States of America, a book on battlefields would touch on events grouped into Revolutionary War and Civil War battles (the latter reaching to Texas, California, and Central Plains states), with a category for "Indian Wars" that would either precede or follow "Civil War" in chronology. All the states bordering the Atlantic and Gulf coasts also would have sections on the War of 1812, and a few East Coast and West Coast states could add "World War II" by stretching the definition of battle to include "attempted attack."

For the land that is now the state of Montana, the situation was different. People who fought within these borders were far away from the United States until the time of the Civil War. The first white settlers in the early 1860s included men who already had served a hitch and were done with battle or who were more interested in personal gain than in politics. They also included men appointed by the U.S. government to run the eastern part of Idaho Territory—from which Montana Territory was carved in 1864. Some of the officials, and a few of the miners, brought along their families. Hordes of merchants and service providers came to profit from the former groups. What Civil War battles Montana saw were fist fights between the half of the population who sympathized with the North and the half who supported the rebels.

So, in Montana, "Indian War" was the only type of battle, and most individual battles clustered in the late 1870s, against one set of Indian allies and one single nation. Even then, only a portion of the Sioux, Northern Cheyenne, Arapaho, and Gros Ventre in one group, and the Nez Perce in the other, was fighting the army in each campaign.

The natives won most of the individual battles, too, but as historian Kermit Edmonds states, theirs were Pyrrhic victories. The U.S. military was able to keep sending soldiers and more soldiers and the food and supplies to keep them going. The army also mounted campaigns during the winter, when native people were used to sheltering from bad weather and getting by on food preserved from the previous year's hunts and trading. In later years, railroads and the resultant settlement combined with the decimation of bison herds finished the battles of Montana's era of "Indian Wars."

Since the early 1900s, service in the U.S. military has been higher per capita among American Indians than in any other ethnic group. In World War II, for example, more than 44,000 native warriors were in the military. Among them were recipients of two Congressional Medals of Honor, fifty-one Silver Stars, thirty-four Distinguished Flying Crosses, forty-seven Bronze Stars, and seventy-one Air Medals. At the end of the twentieth century, Montana's many native veterans ranked the state, with 16 percent of the adult population categorized as veterans, behind only Alaska, and tied Montana with Nevada, Wyoming, and Maine.

Many partisan volumes have been written on most of the battles described here. The current work seeks to tell the stories neutrally, with respect for the men and women on both sides who fought and suffered for ideals and lifestyles they believed were essential. In most situations, combatants on both sides acted honorably according to the teachings of their respective cultures. A few individuals did not.

The reader should keep some things in mind about the setting of the conflicts:

• Montana, North Dakota, South Dakota, and Wyoming did not yet exist as states, and would not until 1889 for the first three (when Dakota Territory was split in half) and the following year for the last.

• Many of the battles and the marches leading to them were in trackless land. In some areas, Indians had developed trails, but primarily rivers and creeks and even seasonally dry creek beds formed the "road system" for finding the way.

• Indian horses in general were smaller and more compact than those the U.S. Army rode. Time and again, these "ponies," as they were often called, could be led to swim rivers while army commanders had to call for engineers to throw down crude bridges, or wait for a contract steamboat to transport troops. Like their riders, army horses did not live off the land as well as the people and the horses that had been there first.

8

• Indian communications among villages meant sending couriers on foot or horseback and awaiting reply by the same means. Army communications in the field also meant sending couriers, either to another unit or to the nearest telegraph station. From there a wire went to the appropriate headquarters, located many states away, which possibly was forwarded to Washington, D.C., for a decision by the army's top general. By the time the reply made its way back to the message sender, days had passed.

Specific divisions of the army discussed in this book, and their headquarters locations in 1876 and 1877, are:

• **U.S. Army**—General of the Army William T. Sherman commanded from headquarters in Washington, D.C.

• **Division of the Missouri**—Major General Philip Sheridan, in Chicago, Illinois, commanded departments that included:

• *Department of the Platte* (the states of Colorado, Iowa, Nebraska, and Wyoming, and Utah Territory)—Brigadier General George Crook, commander in the field from Omaha, Nebraska.

• *Department of Dakota* (the state of Minnesota and Montana, Dakota, and part of Idaho territories), commander: Brigadier General Alfred H. Terry, in the field from St. Paul, Minnesota. Terry's command included the District of Montana, commanded by Colonel John Gibbon, who replaced General Philippe Regis de Trobriand in 1870.

• **Division of the Pacific**—Brigadier General Irvin McDowell, in San Francisco, California, commanded departments that included:

• *Department of the Columbia* (the state of Oregon, and Alaska, Washington, and Idaho territories)—Brigadier General Oliver Otis Howard, commander in the field from Portland, Oregon.

**A note on the maps:** To help readers locate the battlefields detailed in this book, the maps show both historical and contemporary features.

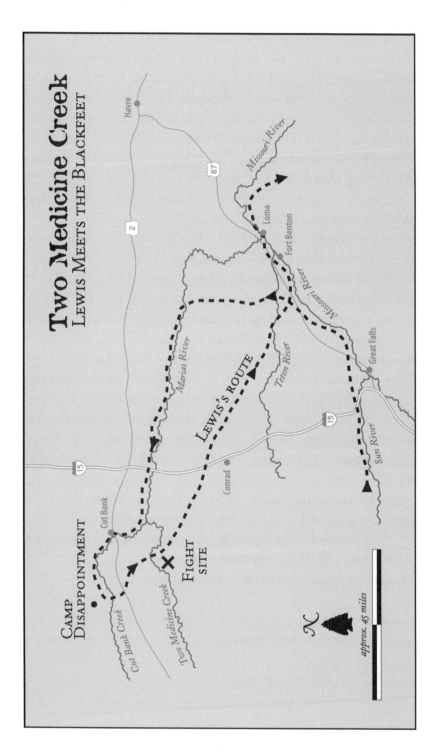

# Two Medicine Creek
## LEWIS MEETS THE BLACKFEET

Havre

Missouri River

87

2

Loma

Fort Benton

Missouri River

Marias River

LEWIS'S ROUTE

Teton River

Great Falls

15

Conrad

Cut Bank

CAMP
DISAPPOINTMENT

FIGHT
SITE

Cut Bank Creek

Two Medicine Creek

Sun River

N

approx. 45 miles

10

# TWO MEDICINE CREEK
## — 1806 —

The Lewis and Clark Expedition of 1803 through 1806 was planned and promoted by President Thomas Jefferson. He talked Congress into funding this first U.S. Army trek into the lands of the Louisiana Purchase, a land acquisition he had long wanted. Because the purchase was defined as all lands drained by the Missouri River and its tributaries, Captain Meriwether Lewis and Captain William Clark were assigned to travel every river mile of the Missouri and map it.

Then, claiming purely scientific reasons, they were to leave the Missouri River drainage at the Continental Divide in the Rocky Mountains and cross to the Columbia River system, which would take them to the Pacific. Besides learning how easy or difficult the mountain crossing was for future commercial use, they would be displaying the American flag in lands that Russian and British traders were visiting regularly, today's states of Washington and Oregon.

Among their day-to-day scientific pursuits, Lewis and Clark accurately recorded wildlife, geography, geology, plants, animals, and birds. When they met Indians, they wrote down vocabulary words to see which languages were related and often wrote about the natives' cultures and beliefs.

Throughout the trip, Lewis and Clark and their band of thirty-some soldiers and contract civilians (joined in spring 1805 by hired interpreters Toussaint Charbonneau, his Shoshone wife, Sacagawea, and their infant boy) also were directed to describe the U.S. government to the natives, urge them to stop warring against traditional enemies, and convince them to turn from British traders to American ones.

The expedition was welcomed by most Indian nations, who shared their precious food, fuel, and labor, as well as valuable information about their home areas. Friendships developed, feasts were held, and evenings were sometimes filled with singing and dancing by hosts and visitors. The Shoshone people sold to the expedition the horses they needed to cross the Rocky Mountains and also helped them carry their gear part of the way. The Nez Perces cared for those horses while the expedition traveled out of their Idaho homeland to the Pacific, where they spent the winter of 1805–1806. Clark became so fond of baby Jean Baptiste Charbonneau that he—with Sacagawea's and Toussaint's permission—raised and educated the boy in St. Louis beginning when he was six years old.

Before the last months of the expedition, Lewis and Clark had had few conflicts with the natives they had encountered. Two episodes of drawn weapons (but no fighting) occurred while they were visiting the Teton Sioux. Later, Lewis and Clark became angry at some winter neighbors on the lower Columbia River, but they did not fight. Those had been the worst situations with Indian people. The only shooting fight between the Lewis and Clark Expedition and a native nation occurred when Meriwether Lewis explored the Marias River in Piegan Blackfeet country. It did not help that Lewis had been primed with stories about the fierceness of the Blackfeet, told by their enemies, and went there expecting trouble.

## Decision Point

During the winter of 1804–1805, while camping at the Mandan and Hidatsa villages at the Knife River on the Missouri, near today's Stanton, North Dakota, Lewis and Clark quizzed the native people about what lay ahead up the Missouri. The Mandans didn't travel far from their farming villages, but the Hidatsas were more adventurous traders and warriors. They described what the expedition could expect well into today's central Montana. One of the major river landmarks mentioned was a waterfall so large it took a whole day to pass around. Not many days' travel after that, the Hidatsas said, the expedition would enter the Rocky Mountains.

Something the Hidatsas had not mentioned, though, came into sight ahead of the boats on June 2, 1805. As they moved upstream, the travelers saw what looked like a fork in the Missouri. Two equally wide streams joined at a point of land near today's Loma. The one from the north was just as muddy as the Missouri River had been all across the plains, but the one from the south ran clear. No one in the party had been here before, but Private Pierre Cruzatte was instantly certain that the muddy "fork" was the true Missouri. He was the best river man in the group, and everyone but the captains agreed with him. Lewis and Clark reasoned that the Missouri's muddiness so far had come from its flowing through the prairie. The river would be clearer near where its snow-fed waters came out of the Rockies.

The disagreement was as close to mutiny as the expedition ever came, but the captains handled it with diplomacy and a clever solution. Before leaving this place, called "Decision Point" today, they had to be certain which was the true Missouri. They had no idea how many weeks it would take to find the Shoshones, buy horses from them, and cross the Rockies, but they knew that this last step had to be completed before snow began piling up in the mountains in the autumn.

Besides, everyone was tired and could use a rest after pushing the canoes against the Missouri's current day after day since April 7. The last few days they had been able to cover only twenty miles against the water. Their army-issue clothing was wearing out, so the men needed to hunt, tan leather, and stitch new clothes. It was decided that Clark would take a small advance party up the south fork and Lewis a small one up the north fork. Each group would travel a day and a half, then return and report whether it had found the landmark waterfalls.

Clark, always a man of his word, followed that schedule and returned to base camp without having seen the falls on the fork the captains thought was the Missouri. Lewis kept his party out two days longer than he should have—alarming the others—and returned having also seen no falls. The enlisted men remained unconvinced.

Lewis said he would take a small group on the south fork and keep on marching until he found the falls. The other men could continue to rest and make the necessary leather moccasins, shirts, and pants.

On June 13, only ten miles past where Clark had turned around, Lewis came upon a waterfall. Wanting to see what the river was like past the falls, he continued upstream alone while the other four men in his group were hunting, away from the river. Within a few miles, he came upon four more waterfalls! What the Hidatsas described as a day's portage would take the expedition two full weeks of carrying all its canoes, gear, and trade goods around the waterfalls.

Lewis named the first falls Great Falls, which eventually became the name of the Montana city built along that stretch of the Missouri.

Back at base camp with news that finally convinced the others which fork was the true Missouri, Lewis named the north fork the Marias River, for his cousin Maria Wood. He and Clark began thinking about exploring the Marias on their return trip. The farther north it began, the farther north the Louisiana Purchase would extend into this fur-rich country.

## In Pahkee Country, 1806

The Shoshones and Nez Perces, who became good friends of expedition members, were traditional enemies of the Piegan Blackfeet. Spending time with the Shoshones and Nez Perces in the fall of 1805 and the spring of 1806, the captains and their men heard many war stories about the Blackfeet. They recorded the tribe's name as "Pahkee," which was actually the Shoshone word for "enemy," and also as "Blackfoot." Both the Shoshones and Nez Perces ventured out onto the plains from their mountain homes only once a year to hunt buffalo, because doing so took them into Blackfeet hunting lands. Often, they joined together for safety in numbers.

When the expedition returned to the future state of Montana over the Lolo Trail in the spring of 1806, they split up. Clark would go east to the Yellowstone River and follow it downstream to its mouth on the Missouri (just east of the present-day Montana–North Dakota border), map it, and evaluate it as a route for commercial shipping.

Lewis planned to go with some men back to the Great Falls, where they would dig up supply caches left in the fall and begin the portage. He would then take an even smaller party overland to the Marias and follow it upstream to its headwaters. There he would make celestial observations to figure longitude and latitude and establish the northernmost edge of the Louisiana Purchase.

Clark would send some of his men downstream on the Missouri to help with the portage around the falls. After completing the portage, those men would camp again at Decision Point, the mouth of the Marias, and await Lewis and his party. Everyone would reunite at the mouth of the Yellowstone on the Missouri sometime in August, they thought.

For his companions on the trip up the Marias, Lewis chose three of the best men in the entire expedition: George Drouillard and brothers Joseph and Reubin Field. Despite the fact that the captains never got any of these men's last names spelled correctly—it was always a phonetic "Drewyer," and "Fields" instead of Field—they obviously respected the men's skills and personalities. Drouillard was of French-Canadian and Shawnee blood and spoke English, French, Shawnee, and Plains Indian Sign. He was a civilian hiree, the expedition's best hunter and tracker, and easily the most valuable member after the two captains. The Field brothers were also excellent hunters and all-around reliable hands, whom Clark had recruited on the Indiana Territory frontier in 1803. The brothers had enlisted in the army as privates.

The party of four left their comrades at the Great Falls on July 16, 1806, and moved cautiously into the Piegan Blackfeet home country. Each had a saddle horse, and two extra horses rounded out the little group. As they drew away from the Missouri River, they saw scattered pronghorns, which Lewis called "goats of this country" or "antelope," and the men were delighted to be "free from the torture of the Musquetoes" (Moulton, p. 112).

Referring to the Blackfeet and the Gros Ventres, Lewis wrote that they "rove through this quarter of the country and as they are a vicious lawless and reather an abandoned set of wretches[,] I wish to avoid an interview with them if possible" (Moulton, p. 113). Such was the impression he had been given by the Blackfeet's enemies. Each night, Lewis took his turn with the other three men in standing guard.

They reached the Marias River on July 19 and rode upstream along it. Two days' travel took them to Cut Bank Creek, which flows from the north to meet Two Medicine Creek and form the Marias. Heading up Cut Bank Creek, they camped about a mile from today's town of Cut Bank at the east edge of the Blackfeet Indian Reservation. On July 22,

Lewis decided there was no point in following the creek farther because its path changed from northerly to southerly. He was the farthest north that the Lewis and Clark Expedition ever went when he set up camp that night to make his celestial observations.

He needed to take multiple readings of star positions, but the weather did not cooperate. Clouds rolled in the next night and hid the moon. Cold, windy, rainy weather lingered for days, and when Lewis and his men finally gave up and left the area on July 26 he labeled the site "Camp Disappointment" (Moulton, p. 127). (Today the actual camp site is on private property.) The four men began moving back toward the Marias to meet the men who had redone the Great Falls portage.

This was the homeland of the Piegan Blackfeet, the southernmost tribe of the Blackfeet Confederacy, which reached south from the Saskatchewan River in present-day Canada.

Before they had horses, Blackfeet men harvested bison by stampeding a herd and guiding it over a cliff called a *pishkun*. It was dangerous but efficient work. At the bottom of the drop, women and children butchered the animals and dried the meat to save for winter. Everyone camped together at the site and ate the choicest pieces of fresh meat. A buffalo hunt was a festive time.

Hunting bison from horseback was also a very dangerous occupation, but safer than driving panicked buffalo on foot. In addition, with horses the Piegans could range farther on their hunts, and the whole village could travel together. Following the buffalo herds could take the Piegans as far south as eastern Idaho. When they met other native nations on the buffalo hunt, Piegan warriors defended their hunting rights.

Women removed the hair from some bison hides and tanned them for leather. Other hides were preserved with the hair still on them to make warm buffalo robes or to cut up for winter moccasins and mittens. The men traded their tobacco crop, meat, hides, finished leather goods, and bison-bone tools for farm products from certain other natives. Blackfeet women and children harvested wild vegetables and fruits in season, preserving them by drying.

In the mid-1750s, British and French-Canadian traders from British fur companies connected with the Piegans. In return for buffalo hides, these white men offered guns and ammunition, metal tools and pots, cloth, flour, coffee, sugar, and whiskey. Piegans also traded with the Kutenai Indians, obtaining beaver pelts that they in turn took to the British posts in present-day Canada and traded—at a profit. The system functioned well, and the Piegans probably saw no reason to change it.

Then a few of the Piegan Blackfeet met the first white men who called themselves "Americans"—Lewis's small group. The following account is based mostly on what Lewis recorded in his journal, the only written record made at the time.

Late on the afternoon of July 27, 1806, Lewis and his party were proceeding along Two Medicine Creek toward its meeting point with Cut Bank Creek. He and the Field brothers had climbed a hill above Two Medicine, while Drouillard was hunting, out of sight, on the creek bottom. Then Lewis noticed "about" thirty horses, half of them saddled, on a hilltop on the far side of the creek, and "several" young Indian men looking down to where Drouillard must be. Half their horses were saddled, Lewis saw, and he at first wrongly assumed that there was a rider for almost every horse. Before the Indian men noticed the Field brothers and himself, Lewis had Joseph unfurl a flag he had brought along. The three began moving slowly toward the Indians—as much to show peaceful intent as to distract them from Drouillard. The Indians seemed "much allarmed" when they noticed the flag-bearers, Lewis reported (Moulton, p. 129).

Lewis believed they were Gros Ventres, also enemies of the Mandans and Hidatsas, of whose warrior abilities he had heard. (Gros Ventre oral history, however, tells that Gros Ventre warriors observed the expedition traveling the Missouri River with a woman in their boats. Since women did not accompany war parties, the Gros Ventres simply ignored these travelers.) Leaving the Field brothers, Lewis approached the warriors and began shaking hands; the Field brothers came and did the same. Doing his best in sign language, Lewis said that he wanted to smoke and talk with them, but could not until his other man, Drouillard, joined them. Reubin Field and one of the young Indian men left to find Drouillard.

Meanwhile Lewis presented a medal, a flag, and a handkerchief to the three men he thought were being introduced as chiefs and suggested that everyone camp together overnight. (This location is also currently private property.) He said he was "glad to see them and had a great deel [sic] to say to them" (Moulton, p. 130).

Drouillard soon returned, and camp was set up on Two Medicine Creek. The Piegans built a half-dome with brush and threw buffalo robes over it for their shelter, inviting the white men to share it. Lewis and Drouillard accepted the hospitality that night and the Field brothers slept nearby at the campfire.

But during the evening, through Drouillard's Plains Indian Sign, Lewis learned what he could about the young Indian men and where they were from. With none of the white men able to speak the language, Lewis did not record the men's names. They smoked and "talked," and Lewis learned that the men came from a large village that was moving toward the mouth of the Marias River en route to a British trading post on the North Saskatchewan River in Canada.

An abbreviated form of the standard speech that Lewis had given (and Drouillard and the Field brothers had heard) dozens of times by now came out in signs. He said he was from a new government that now controlled this land, one that wanted to befriend the native people. Its leader, President Jefferson, wanted the native nations to make peace with one another. Lewis explained that he himself had already visited with the Arikaras, Hidatsas, Mandans, Shoshones, Nez Perces, and others, and everyone had agreed to this. The president also wanted the natives to stop trading with the British and welcome American traders, who would bring guns and any other desired goods.

Unfortunately, sign language was better suited for trading than discussing abstract political concepts. Drouillard was reported to be quite fluent in sign, but the Piegans thought the message was: The new government, which wants you to abandon trading with your longtime friends, has made allies out of your enemies, who are also joined as one, and will be trading guns to them. Because each tribe was identified by a unique sign, the Piegans had no doubt about the specific enemy tribes Lewis named. Certainly it was an arrogant or just plain rude thing to say.

Realizing that these men were not chiefs, Lewis also invited them to get their "head chiefs" and come to the mouth of the Marias River where they could meet with Lewis and more of his men, who would be waiting there. Both Lewis and Clark, like military officers later in the nineteenth century, believed that native governments were organized like their own. Somewhere was the equivalent of a "president" over these men, and Lewis wanted to meet him. He promised that those who visited the Marias would receive gifts of horses and tobacco.

## "Let Go My Gun!"

Before everyone turned in for the night, Lewis organized a guard. He took first watch, then Reubin Field went on duty and Lewis "fell into a profound sleep and did not wake until the noise…awoke me a little after light in the morning" (Moulton, p. 132).

Joseph Field was the guard by then, but he "had carelessly laid his gun down" near where Reubin was sleeping (Moulton, p. 133). When the Piegans awoke and gathered at the campfire, one man picked up the Field brothers' guns and two other men took those of the still-sleeping Drouillard and Lewis. Joseph shouted for Reubin, and the two chased the Piegans for "50 or 60 paces from the camp." In seizing the guns, Reubin stabbed one Piegan "to the heart," and that man ran a few more steps, fell, and died (Moulton, p. 134).

Drouillard had just awakened when he saw the Piegan man pick up his gun, and he shouted, "Damn you! Let go my gun!" That woke Lewis, who reached for his rifle just as he saw one of the Piegans running away with it. He drew his single-shot pistol and ran after him. Seeing the gun, the man was just putting down Lewis's rifle when the Field brothers came back from their chase and took aim to shoot him. Lewis forbade them from doing so. Drouillard arrived and also suggested killing the Piegans, but Lewis again refused.

The Piegans turned their attention to driving off the white men's six horses up Two Medicine Creek. Lewis and the others again ran after them, Lewis shouting as he ran that he would not shoot them if they released the horses. For "three hundred paces" they continued, until Lewis was "nearly out of breath" (Moulton, p. 134).

One of the Piegans took cover in the rocks while the others "spoke to each other" and turned to face Lewis. He reacted by shooting one of them—who still wore the Peace Medal that Lewis had given him the night before—"through the belly." The man went down but raised himself partially and fired at Lewis as he "crawled in behind a rock" (Moulton, p. 134). Lewis "felt the wind of his bullet very distinctly" (Moulton, p. 135). Whether this man survived his wound is unclear.

Without his shot pouch, Lewis could not reload, so he returned to the campsite, meeting Drouillard, who had been running to his aid at the sound of the shots. Leaving the Field brothers to pursue the horses, Lewis and Drouillard quickly caught the horses that had remained at the campsite and packed their gear. After the brothers returned with four of the horses purchased from the Shoshones the previous autumn, Lewis decided to take four of the best Piegan horses.

In a fury, he also set fire to all the warriors' baggage, which had been left at the camp: four shields, two bows, arrow-filled quivers, and "sundry other articles." He took one gun that the Piegans had left behind and the gift flag, but left the Peace Medal on the dead man "that they might be informed who we were" (Moulton, p. 135). Lewis noted in his journal that the Piegans had at least two guns and several horses among them—including two of his own—that would get them back to their village.

One story in the Blackfeet oral tradition says that these Piegans were adolescent boys learning and practicing warrior skills for future use. In what was a rite of passage, they had been capturing horses from an enemy village and were on their way home. If they had failed in their stealth at that village, they likely would have been insulted and humiliated and then sent home—not killed. That fateful morning by the shared campfire, their leader challenged them to take something from the white men's camp as part of the practice raid.

It also was Blackfeet custom that people who camped together shared all their provisions and equipment.

Another story, recorded by army 1st Lieutenant James H. Bradley seven decades later, says that the young men had tried to practice their horse-capturing skills on Lewis's camp that night, after the evening visit but before dawn. Two were caught and held hostage for the return of the missing horses. When they tried to escape the next morning, they were killed.

Lewis and his men had "no doubt" (Moulton, p. 136) that the Piegans would send out a larger war party as soon as they heard about the fight—perhaps bypassing Lewis's tiny group and heading straight for the larger party that Lewis had freely said would be at the mouth of the Marias. Either way, the four believed they had to get away from Two Medicine Creek quickly and reach the Marias before any Piegans did.

They mounted up and pushed their "horses as hard as they would bear" until three o'clock that afternoon. They rode southeast, past the site of present-day Conrad and on to the Teton River, where they stopped for an hour and a half to rest, eat, and let the horses graze. Pressing on from 4:30 P.M. until "dark" meant another six or seven hours in the saddle, at which time they stopped again, killed a bison, and ate. After the moon rose, they continued, but more slowly, until about 2:00 A.M. By then they were not far west of where Fort Benton would be built on the Missouri River forty-four years later, and "much fatiegued as may be readily conceived" (Moulton, p. 136).

Daylight awakened them in a few hours, with Lewis "so soar from [his] ride yesterday that [he] could scarcely stand, and the men complained of being in a similar situation…" (Moulton, p. 137).

They rode on, hearing a few gunshots as they finally neared the Missouri. Instead of a Piegan war party, the gunshots belonged to the expected Ordway party, some just pulling up in five canoes and some arriving a little later on horseback. Everyone who had planned to meet at the Marias was once again together. They quickly dug up the food and supply caches left the previous year, finding some items good and some spoiled, but they were unable to locate three traps belonging to Drouillard. Lewis, however, did not want to stay and search any longer. The combined Lewis and Ordway parties set off downstream in the canoes and the one pirogue that had survived its winter storage.

The Lewis and Clark Expedition's record of peaceful contact with dozens of native nations now stood blemished by the few moments on Two Medicine Creek. And the Piegan Blackfeet were not impressed with these new white men who called themselves "Americans."

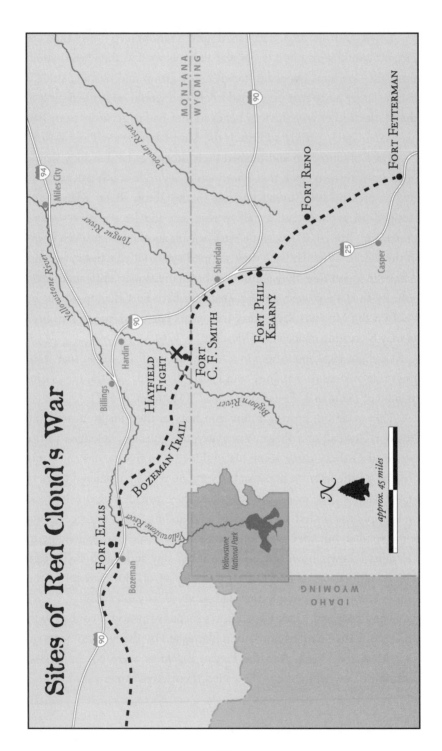

# Sites of Red Cloud's War

MONTANA
WYOMING

Powder River

Miles City

Tongue River

Yellowstone River

Sheridan

Hardin

Billings

Bighorn River

HAYFIELD
FIGHT

FORT
C. F. SMITH

BOZEMAN TRAIL

FORT ELLIS

Yellowstone River

Bozeman

Yellowstone
National Park

FORT PHIL
KEARNY

FORT RENO

FORT FETTERMAN

Casper

IDAHO
WYOMING

N

approx. 45 miles

# THE HAYFIELD FIGHT
# — 1867 —

Only a few white men visited present-day Montana after the Lewis and Clark Expedition, mostly to trap or trade with the native residents. Gold discoveries on Gold Creek and Grasshopper Creek in far western Montana between 1858 and 1862 changed that. Prospectors began rushing east from California and west on the Oregon Trail, which ran across Nebraska and southern Wyoming, then turned north for Montana. Speed was imperative because they could cross the plains during the brief summers. The same was true for supplies that pioneering merchants stocked to serve the gold seekers.

In 1863, John M. Bozeman and John Jacobs created the Bozeman Trail, which headed north from the Oregon Trail near today's Douglas, Wyoming. Livestock grazing opportunities and water were scarce along much of its route, but the Bozeman "cut-off" became the fastest way to Montana gold. Bozeman and Jacobs found plenty of emigrants eager to pay for their guide services and take chances in rushing to the mining camps.

The Lakota, or Teton Sioux, people—one of the three linguistic and regional divisions in the Sioux Nation—had lived on the upper Great Plains for about three centuries. The Dakota, or Santee, Sioux had remained in today's Minnesota, and the Nakota, or Yankton, Sioux followed bison in present-day southern South Dakota and northern Nebraska (Hoxie, p. 590). ("Sioux" was the Ojibwa word for "little snakes," as recorded by French traders in the mid-seventeenth century.) Under pressure from Ojibwas (Chippewas) and being pushed westward by white settlement, the Lakotas left Minnesota and Wisconsin and became nomadic bison hunters ranging from Nebraska and Kansas through western Dakota, eastern Wyoming, and Montana. After the

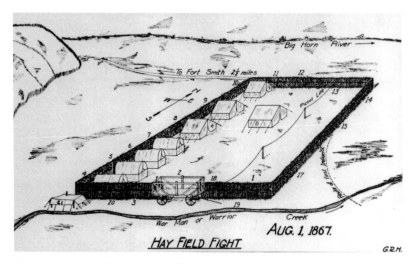

Map and drawing of the area and positions of combatants involved in the Hayfield Fight.

horse arrived on the northern plains, they became even more powerful.

Like the Blackfeet, they did not farm, but harvested wild fruits and vegetables and traded meat and hides for the produce of farming tribes. Their conical lodges, made of hides stretched over wooden poles, were aerodynamically sound, cozy structures that withstood the intense winds on the unforested plains. These tipis also could be taken down quickly, with the poles used to make triangular frames for "travois," as French trappers called the horse-drawn sledges that carried all the household goods. If in danger, a Lakota village could move fifty miles in a day, but an average day's travel was less than fifteen miles.

The Lakota Sioux people were divided into seven tribes who lived separately in winter and combined in various bands for summer buffalo hunting, meat and hide processing, and visiting. These tribes were the Oglala, Brulé, Hunkpapa, Minneconjou, Sans Arc, Sihasapa, and Two Kettles (Hoxie, p. 591). Some members of each group except the Two Kettles would be at the village on the Little Bighorn River in June 1876, but the majority there were Oglala, Hunkpapa, and Minnecoujou.

Worse than the new Bozeman Trail's lack of grass and water was its path right through Powder River country, which included some of the Lakotas', Arapahos', and Northern Cheyennes' favorite bison-hunting places in southeastern Montana and eastern Wyoming. When the old mountain man Jim Bridger heard about the Bozeman Trail's location, he said only fools would use it. During the six seasons of the trail's existence, Indians under the great Sioux military tactician Red Cloud regularly attacked travelers on the "Bloody Bozeman." When the army built five forts along the trail to protect travelers, Indians attacked them, too. In the trail's final season, raiding Blackfeet killed John Bozeman on his namesake trail. The efforts of the Lakota Sioux, called Red Cloud's War, succeeded in 1868, when the U.S. Army closed the trail and abandoned its forts (except for Fort Fetterman in Wyoming). The Sioux promptly burned the abandoned posts.

Fort C. F. Smith, built in 1866 on the north side of the Bighorn River across from today's town of Fort Smith and the Bighorn Canyon National Recreation Area, was one of two Montana forts on the Bozeman Trail. Fort Ellis, then four miles east of Bozeman, was the second. The Wyoming forts were Fort Fetterman (1867), east of Casper on the North Platte River at the start of the Bozeman Trail; Fort Reno (1865), at the trail's Powder River crossing southwest of Gillette; and Fort Phil Kearny (1866), south of Sheridan.

For army men, assignment to the isolated posts north of Fort Fetterman was truly hardship duty. Snowbound in the winter, the men had to be self-sufficient in order to survive. At Fort Smith, that included

*Chief Gall, 1880. Photograph by D. F. Barry.*
COURTESY MONTANA HISTORICAL SOCIETY.

raising their own hay for cavalry horses. The hayfield at Fort Smith (today on private property) was too far from the fort for the men to ride out, work, and return daily. Troops built an encampment at the field, surrounded by a log-and-brush fence. Detachments took turns staying on-site to cut the hay and spread it out to cure.

In 1867, nineteen soldiers and six civilians, under the command of 2nd Lieutenant Sigismund Sternberg, were staying and working at the hayfield camp at harvest time. With them was a herd of twenty-nine mules and three horses. At 9:00 A.M. on August 1, about seven hundred Sioux warriors attacked. Two soldiers were killed immediately and another would be mortally wounded in the hours to come.

The Sioux shot flaming arrows into the fence, setting fire to the dry prairie grass on three sides of the encampment. Amid the smoke and gunfire, the soldiers managed to extinguish the fires inside the enclosure. The prairie was not yet dry enough to blaze through camp. The soldiers and civilians managed to hold off their attackers all day long, although three more men were wounded. Their main advantage over the Sioux was new and better guns—rapid-firing (though single-shot), breech-loading 50-caliber Springfield rifles and repeating rifles. The Sioux had first encountered these the year before in the Wagon Box Fight near Fort Phil Kearny in Wyoming. There they had expected soldiers to need the usual thirty seconds or more to reload after each shot. While soldiers reloaded, the Indians would continue their charges. But surprisingly, soldiers at the Wagon Box shot continually.

When the Indians decided to withdraw at about 5:00 P.M., only one of the camp's three horses and one of its twenty-nine mules had survived. Amazingly, however, twenty-two of the defending force had lived through an attack by an Indian force many times their numbers.

The Hayfield Fight was the single Montana Territory battle in what is known as Red Cloud's War.

## Red Cloud's War

That same year of 1867, the federal government instituted its Peace Policy, a plan to move all native peoples onto reservations managed by civilians rather than the military. Natives would receive food and supplies, education, and Christian religious training while learning to become self-supporting farmers. A treaty between the government and each Indian nation established each reservation and how long its annuities would continue. Churches sent missionaries and teachers, and the government hired white civilians as Indian agents to administer reservation programs.

None of this made sense to the nomadic Plains Indians. Chief Gall of the Hunkpapa Sioux clearly outlined their position to a Peace Commission at Fort Rice in today's South Dakota, in 1867:

> *This is our land and our home. We have no exact boundaries, but the graves of the Sioux Nation mark our possessions. Wherever they are found the land is ours. We were born naked, and have been taught to hunt and live on the game. You tell us that we must learn to farm, live in one house, and take on your ways. Suppose the people living beyond the great sea would come and tell you that you must stop farming and kill your cattle, and take your houses and lands, what would you do? Would you not fight them?* (Vaughn, Reynolds Campaign, p. 124)

In 1868, when the U.S. government admitted defeat in Red Cloud's War, it negotiated a treaty at Fort Laramie, which closed the Bozeman Trail and its three forts north of Fort Fetterman. The Indians won only a partial victory, though, because the Fort Laramie Treaty of 1868 actually cut down on land marked as theirs in the previous Fort Laramie Treaty of 1851.

The old treaty had reserved to the Sioux the land extending north of the North Platte River in western Nebraska to the Missouri River in Montana. Its 1868 successor established the Great Sioux Reservation as the western half of today's South Dakota—from the Missouri River to the Wyoming border—plus the northwestern corner of Nebraska. The 1868 treaty said that all the Sioux and Northern Cheyennes must now move onto the Great Sioux Reservation. Later, the Northern Cheyennes were to be moved to present-day Oklahoma. They were to join the Southern Cheyennes, from whom they had voluntarily split before 1830 (Hoxie, p. 113), on their reservation.

Some Sioux and Northern Cheyenne leaders rejected the 1868

*Sitting Bull. No date, photograph by D. F. Barry.*

treaty and believed that not signing left them free to continue following the bison herds. Among these "nontreaty" people were Sioux led by Sitting Bull, Gall and, in war, Crazy Horse, and Northern Cheyennes led by Dull Knife and Little Wolf, including Two Moon's band. Many of the approximately 3,400 nontreaty people were willing to trade with white men for guns, ammunition, cloth, whiskey, and other manufactured goods. They definitely were not interested in farming small plots of land.

Other Sioux leaders— 159 chiefs from ten bands— did sign the 1868 treaty, and they and approximately 11,000 people moved onto the Great Sioux Reservation. Notable among them were Red Cloud himself and the Brulé leader, Spotted Tail.

One of the treaty's flaws was creating the unceded lands—mostly in Montana Territory's southeastern corner. These important hunting lands were neither assigned to a reservation nor designated for white settlement. Indians could hunt on them as long as buffalo remained. The nontreaty Sioux interpreted this to mean that the lands continued to be theirs—the thousands of square miles where the Bighorn, Rosebud, Tongue, and Powder rivers flowed north into the Yellowstone.

Nontreaty Sioux, Northern Cheyennes, and Arapahos continued to live and move around the area in the traditional way. For nearly a decade, when summer came, nearly half of the treaty people left the reservation to join the nontreaty people. Everyone moved the villages to follow bison during the hunting season, tan hides, dry meat, and visit friends and relatives. The treaty people then returned to the reservation for the winter—not what the authors of the Peace Policy had intended. These two groups would become the targets for the Great Sioux War of 1876 and 1877, which began with the ultimatum that the Indian people stay on the reservation except when given permits to leave.

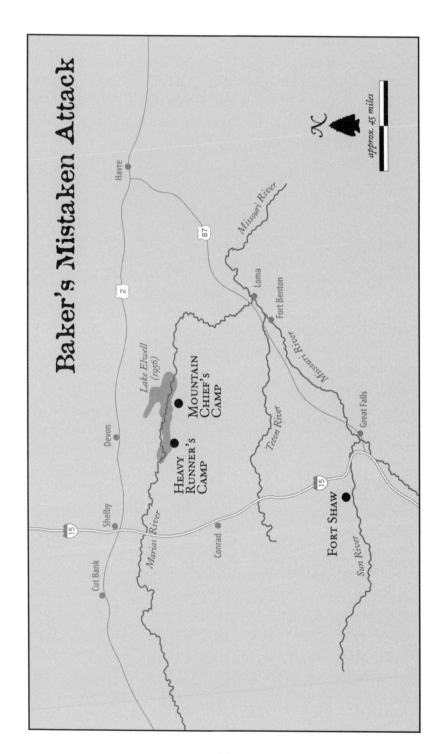

# Baker's Mistaken Attack

# MARIAS MASSACRE
## — 1870 —

Conditions were terrible in the Piegan village of Chief Heavy Runner at dawn on January 23, 1870. The temperature hovered at forty degrees below zero and many people were sick with smallpox, aching with high fevers and covered with scarring sores. But at least the sick were being cared for by their families at a favorite Marias River wintering site (south of today's Devon and now under the waters of Lake Elwell).

The warriors of the camp were away hunting for fresh meat, but the village was safely far from white men and any troubles with them— like the incident four months ago with the Clarke family. Besides, Heavy Runner had a government certificate acknowledging him and his village as friendly to the United States.

The Piegans had reluctantly given up trading with British fur companies—exchanging beaver pelts and buffalo hides for guns, ammunition, and other goods—when the United States moved in. At first they had fought the American trappers who pushed into the area. But when the newcomers finally started trading in the familiar British way (assigning points for pelts) at Fort Piegan in 1832, the relationship improved. Many Piegans began going to this post on the Missouri River at the mouth of the Marias River (at today's Loma) to trade.

One of the men the American Fur Company sent to Piegan country was Malcolm Clarke, the only son of a career army officer, who had spent his early childhood at Minnesota frontier forts. An intelligent young man, he was appointed to the U.S. Military Academy's Class of 1838, but his fiery temper led to several fist fights and finally to a challenge to a duel with a classmate. He was kicked out of the military academy. In the early 1840s, he arrived in present-day Montana employed by American Fur and soon was in charge of its Marias River operations.

31

Clarke married into the Piegan tribe, taking as his bride a woman named Kahkokima, Cutting Off Head Woman, a chief's daughter. Initially his in-laws called him "White Lodgepole" for his build, then Clarke earned the name "Four Bears" when he killed four grizzlies in one day. Kahkokima and Four Bears' family grew with the births of sons Horace and Nathan and daughters Helen and Isabel. Helen later wrote that her father was a "stern disciplinarian" but not "a tyrant."

The American Fur Company and the great era of fur trading ended at about the same time the gold finds began in southwestern Montana. The Clarke family moved to the Prickly Pear Valley, north of Helena, where Malcolm started a stock farm on Little Prickly Pear Creek near Wolf Creek. Being on the main Helena to Fort Benton road soon made Malcolm well known in Helena, twenty-five miles south.

Mrs. Clarke's relatives were always welcome at the Clarke ranch, and they regularly came for lengthy stays. Her cousin Ne-tus-che-o, called Pete Owl Child by whites, brought his wife, mother, sister, and younger brother for such a visit in the spring of 1867.

Something, however, went wrong during this visit, which created bad blood between Owl Child and the Clarke men. One story says that some of Owl Child's horses were stolen from the ranch by white settlers, but the Clarkes refused to try to find them. Another story says that while Owl Child and Horace Clarke were out hunting, Malcolm made improper advances to Owl Child's wife. Whatever happened to start the quarrel, when the Owl Child party left the ranch, they took some of the Clarkes' horses and a small telescope. Malcolm and Horace tracked them all the way to a Piegan village on the Teton River, where Malcolm knocked Owl Child off a Clarke horse and reclaimed his property. This insult was witnessed by the whole village.

## Incident at the Clarke Ranch

More than two years later, on August 17, 1869, Owl Child and four other young Piegan men—Black Weasel, Eagle's Rib, Bear Chief, and Black Bear—arrived at the Clarke ranch on a fine summer evening. Nathan, Clarke's younger son at age fourteen, was away looking for lost horses. Helen and her father were playing a game of backgammon. Helen greeted her cousin Owl Child by teasing that "our horses are being stolen." She, her mother and sister, and aunt Black Bear (named the same as one of the visitors) began preparing a meal. Owl Child hugged fifteen-year-old Horace in greeting. Owl Child smoked with Malcolm, explaining that he was returning horses some Blood Indians from Canada had captured from Clarke a few years ago. In addition, Owl Child had a message to deliver from Mountain Chief, who was inviting Malcolm to come and trade at his village. Black Weasel was his son.

Mountain Chief had hated most whites since three men had shot his brother in Fort Benton and nothing had been done about it. The murder was in retaliation for a wagon train attack by non-Piegans. Mountain Chief had banned all whites from his village, but he stayed friendly toward Malcolm Clarke because of his marriage to Kahkokima.

Helen later said that she believed the young men with Owl Child acted strangely nervous. Even when asked to eat, they were reluctant to enter the house, then moved around restlessly, picking up and inspecting ornaments. Nevertheless, when Horace started for the stockyard with Bear Chief to look at the returned horses but could not find his gun, Helen told him he was safe with friends and did not need it. The time was about midnight, and the guests were saying they had to leave soon.

Outside, Bear Chief shot Horace in the head and left him for dead. Hearing the gunshot, Malcolm flew out the door, and Eagle's Rib shot him through the heart. Twenty-five or so young warriors now rode out of the woods, shouting, and then galloped away.

Then the women heard Horace's cry for help. The bullet had entered his right nostril and exited behind his left cheekbone. He was a gory sight and would be permanently disfigured. Aunt Black Bear and Helen dragged him into the house. The four women hid with him in a bedroom as the mounted warriors returned. They entered the house and began to destroy it, dumping food on the floor and stealing what they wanted. When Aunt Black Bear boldly left the bedroom to dress them down, they took her hostage and rode away. She escaped after a few miles and went to the nearby ranch of Joe Cobell, whose

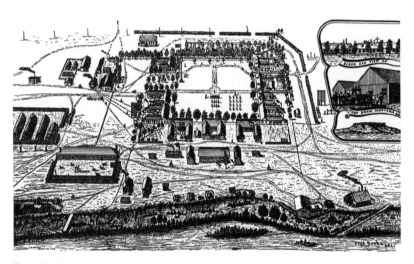

*Letterhead showing Fort Shaw. Pencil sketch by Fred Brown. Date unknown.*
COURTESY MONTANA HISTORICAL SOCIETY.

second wife, Mary, was a sister of Mountain Chief (Cobell's first wife also had been Piegan).

At dawn, Helen and Isabel sent a ranch hand into Helena and went to another nearby ranch for help. Their mother was in shock and helpless. The neighboring Wilkinsons gave the sisters food and medical supplies for Horace, but were afraid to go back with them. Nathan returned from his horse-hunting trip in the afternoon to discover the sad news. Late in the day, several prominent Helena men, friends of Malcolm, arrived and put the house in order. They buried Malcolm the following day.

In October, Helen and the scarred Horace testified before a Helena grand jury that indicted all five of the Piegan men for murder. U.S. Marshal William F. Wheeler served the indictment on Montana Territory's Superintendent of Indian Affairs, General Alfred Sully, who passed it to Commissioner of Indian Affairs John Q. Smith in Washington, D.C. Smith replied with orders for Sully to demand that the Piegan chiefs turn in the men for trial.

On January 1, 1870, Sully and Wheeler traveled to the Blackfeet Indian Agency (then at today's Choteau) and met with several friendly Piegan chiefs, including Heavy Runner. The Piegan leaders said that the indicted men had gone to stay for a while with relatives in Canada.

In the weeks after Clarke's murder, a band of twenty or so young Piegans made several raids on Benton Road travelers. They were assumed to be the same group that had vandalized the Clarke home in August 1869. While General Sully was seeking a nonmilitary solution to the problem, General Philippe Regis de Trobriand wrote to Division of the Missouri head Philip Sheridan that the answer was to attack Mountain Chief's village. De Trobriand commanded Montana army forts from headquarters at Fort Shaw on the Sun River, west of Great Falls.

Sheridan sent his own inspector from Chicago to Montana. James Hardie interviewed people like Joe Cobell and Joe Kipp (a French Canadian–Mandan trader), both of whom spoke Piegan and knew the villages and their chiefs. Hardie soon agreed with De Trobriand and wired Sheridan, "Question is, whether chastisement or capture for hostages should be the principal design." In reply Sheridan wrote, "If the lives and property of citizens of Montana can be protected by striking Mountain Chief's band, I want them struck. Tell Baker to strike them hard."

## Baker in the Field

Major Eugene M. Baker commanded Fort Ellis near Bozeman. He was a West Point graduate who had served with distinction during the Civil War.

Baker selected four companies of the Second Cavalry stationed at Fort Ellis. They marched to Fort Shaw, arriving on January 14, where Baker met with De Trobriand, Hardie, Cobell, and Kipp. The latter two would go along as interpreters and to make sure that Baker identified the correct village. Baker was to arrest not only the five men indicted for Clarke's murder, but also Mountain Chief and thirteen others suspected of attacks on white settlers.

Fearing that Mountain Chief's people would flee north to Canada, the military men agreed on night marches. Cobell and Kipp located good places for hidden daytime campsites. Clarke's two sons were allowed to join the civilian teamsters and volunteers. Also added to Baker's cavalry command were fifty-five mounted troops of the Thirteenth Infantry and supply wagons managed by trader Paul McCormick.

The force left Fort Shaw on January 19, the mid-morning temperature of minus-thirty forcing the soldiers to wrap blankets and buffalo robes over their wool uniforms. Snow in their path was one to two feet deep. Four days later, near daylight, they reached the sleeping, smallpox-infected, forty-four–lodge village of Chief Heavy Runner. It was on the site occupied by Mountain Chief's camp the week previously, when Kipp had scouted the area. Baker called for silence as his troops prepared to attack.

Suddenly Joe Kipp ran to Baker shouting that he recognized Heavy Runner's lodge and that this was the wrong village. The major ordered his soldiers to shoot Kipp if he yelled again.

Almost at the same time, Chief Heavy Runner ran from his lodge, waving his government certificate. Without orders, someone fired a shot, killing him, and the troops took that as the signal to begin firing. (Years later, Joe Cobell said he had killed Heavy Runner to protect his wife's relatives; others say it was because of captured horses.) According to the army, some Piegans rushed out of their lodges and hid in the brush, firing back. One woman, Holy Medicine Bear Woman, wrapped herself and two children in a buffalo robe and rolled them downhill away from camp to safety.

Civilian interpreter Thomas H. LeForge later recounted that soldiers freely killed women and children. During the shooting he came upon a young mother,

> hidden in the brush, nursing her baby. She jumped up, in great fear. She made signs…saying, "Wait until my baby gets its fill from my breast. Then you may kill me. But let the baby live, I give it to you." She held the infant out toward me. I ignored her, turned aside and went away. A little while later I again passed that thicket. There I saw the dead bodies of both the mother and child. (Gibson and Hayne)

The troops shot into the village for about an hour before charging into it with sabers drawn, to destroy the lodges and contents, including food, and capture the Piegans' pony herd.

*Marching from stables at Fort Ellis, 1888. After being decommissioned in 1886, the fort saw occasional use by National Guard troops. Photographer unidentified.*

After the shooting was over, Baker learned that Mountain Chief's village was a few miles away. Leaving 1st Lieutenant Gustavus Doane and one company at Heavy Runner's village, Baker took the rest of his troops down the Marias, but found Mountain Chief's campsite abandoned.

Doane's official count was 173 dead Piegans, 120 of them, he said, "able men." But Kipp wrote, in 1913, that he himself counted 217 dead and that the only shot the Piegans fired was one by a wounded warrior who killed Sergeant Walter McKay when he looked inside the Piegan man's lodge before starting to tear it down. McKay's was the only army death; another man suffered a broken leg when his horse fell. More than one hundred Piegans were taken captive temporarily, then released and given a supply of army hardtack and bacon. In the terrific cold and deep snows, they walked ninety-some miles overland to Fort Benton, some of the people dying along the way.

Baker left troops with Lieutenant Doane to finish destroying the village and marched the others down the Marias to find Mountain Chief's village, but its residents had fled to Canada. Mountain Chief died there two years later in a hunting accident.

# Policy Change

Marching in constant subzero temperatures, Baker's battalion returned to Fort Shaw and De Trobriand's congratulations on January 29, then rested a day and left on January 31 to arrive back at Fort Ellis on February 5. It took Baker another dozen days to get around to filing his official report.

More quickly, though, the Piegans' Indian agent, 1st Lieutenant William B. Pease, reported to his boss, General Sully, what he had learned from village survivors. They said that 148 of the 173 killed were women, children, and elders because few warriors were in the village when it was attacked. Sully signed the report and forwarded it to Commissioner of Indian Affairs Smith. The United States at the time was still debating the government's Peace Policy towards Indian peoples, which had begun three years before. News of what soon was called the Marias Massacre became oil on that fire. President Grant soon announced that all Indian agents now would be civilians rather than military officers. Later in the decade, though, he would reverse his policy again to favor the military.

Not surprisingly, General William Sherman issued a press release referring to Pease's document as "absurd . . . [in saying] that there were only thirteen [sic] warriors killed and that all the balance were women and children, more or less afflicted with smallpox" (Gibson and Hayne). He did ask Baker for a follow-up report, which the major finally wrote on March 23—two months afterward—merely confirming his first statement.

Horace Clarke, who had gone with Baker seeking revenge for his father's death, spoke more than once against the major's actions and in defense of Heavy Runner. Under oath, he testified to the Indian Claims Commission in 1920 that he, Horace,

> *was in the Baker fight and personally knew Heavy Runner, a good Indian and a friend of the white people. His camp was practically wiped out....Those who were not killed were left homeless and penniless. Thirteen hundred head of horses and several thousand buffalo robes were taken from the people. It is an undeniable fact*

*that Col. [sic] Baker was drunk and did not know what he was doing. (Gibbon and Hayne)*

The army ignored such claims in 1870, and did not court-martial Baker, although generals Sully and De Trobriand were reassigned and subsequently left Montana. But Baker was left in place at Fort Ellis to cause more problems.

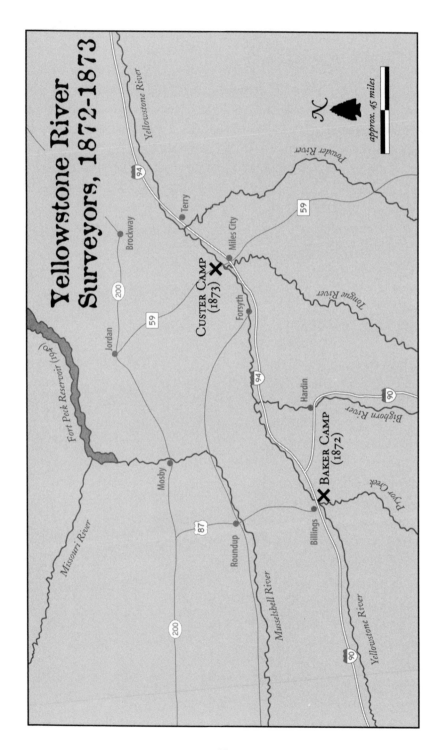

Yellowstone River Surveyors, 1872-1873

# CUSTER AND CRAZY HORSE MEET
## — 1872 —

Major Eugene Baker figured in another battle against Montana natives only two years after the Marias Massacre. By then, the nontreaty Sioux had begun regular attacks to halt railroad building along the Yellowstone River, which ran right through the heart of their unceded hunting lands. Well before Northern Pacific Railroad construction crews could move into the area, the route had to be surveyed and laid out. The Sioux considered the survey crews and their military escorts fair game in the battle to stop the railroad.

Prominent geologist Ferdinand V. Hayden had surveyed the Yellowstone River's course for the federal government in 1871, work that helped get Yellowstone National Park designated the following year. In the summers of 1872 and 1873, the graduate of Oberlin College and Albany Medical School oversaw the Northern Pacific's work to plot its rail line along the lower Yellowstone.

Sioux leaders Sitting Bull and Gall—and other nontreaty Sioux, Northern Cheyennes, and Arapahos—apparently believed that attacking any workers creating the railroad would help stop the project. They did not want the noisy, dirty steam engines driving away the vast bison herds that were central to Sioux culture. They also knew that white settlers—including post traders who sold the whiskey that Sitting Bull so strongly opposed—would appear in the rail line's wake. Towns and ranch fences would close hunting lands essential to their way of living.

This, of course, was just what the army hoped for. Its leaders were only too glad to supply military escorts for Hayden's surveyors. But Major Baker being in command of the 1872 escort nearly proved fatal for soldiers and surveyors alike, and boosted Sitting Bull's and Crazy Horse's confidence that they could beat the white men.

## Baker with the Northern Pacific

In 1871, survey crews began three summers of laying out the Northern Pacific Railroad's route up the Yellowstone River. The following year, two survey teams worked toward each other in the unceded lands. The eastern crew worked upstream on the Yellowstone from its mouth on the Missouri River. Beginning at the mouth of the Shields River, at today's Livingston, the western team surveyed down the Yellowstone. The two were to meet approximately at the mouth of the Powder River, near today's Terry.

Each crew had a military escort. As General of the Army, William T. Sherman told Congress in March 1872: "This railroad is a national enterprise, and we are forced to protect the men during its survey and construction, through, probably, the most warlike nation of Indians on this continent, who will fight for every foot of the line." The federal government did not lend the Northern Pacific any money as it had the Union Pacific and others. But the Northern Pacific received land grants totaling thirty-nine million acres, the largest ever for any U.S. railroad.

*John Gibbon. No date, photograph by D. F. Barry.* COURTESY MONTANA HISTORICAL SOCIETY.

Colonel John Gibbon, who had replaced De Trobriand as commander of the army's District of Montana at Fort Shaw, assigned Major Baker to command the western survey crew's military escort of about 370 troops: Companies C, E, G, and I of the Seventh Infantry, and Companies F, G, H, and L of the Second Cavalry. Beginning at the Shields River on July 30, 1872, the men worked uneventfully for about two weeks. The night of August

13–14 found them camped on the Yellowstone's south side at the mouth of Pryor Creek, east of Billings. (The site is on private property, but at the time this book went to press, negotiations were underway for public access to and interpretation at a vantage point overlooking the battle-field.)

The Yellowstone River has since changed course and no longer borders the location, but in 1872 2nd Lieutenant Edward J. McClernand of the Second Cavalry described the camp as being

> within a slough that, with the river, entirely surrounded the camp ground. This slough was fringed with large cottonwoods and at the lower end, extending some seventy-five yards from the river, there was also a thick growth of tall willow brush. Pickets were posted along the slough, and the wagons, perhaps a hundred in number, were parked in the form of an ellipse with one end open, so as to form a corral into which the wagon mules, left out to graze during the night, could be driven if necessary. (McClernand, p. 30)

This bivouac was northeast of the Crow Indians' home country, where their reservation formed the western boundary of the unceded lands. The Crows and the Sioux were traditional enemies who regularly raided each other's villages, capturing horses to insult and impoverish the other tribe while gaining honor and wealth for the victorious warrior and his tribe. This tradition, like that of counting coup (touching but not killing an enemy during battle), was an important and respectable part of Plains Indian warfare.

A war party of Sioux, Northern Cheyenne, and Arapaho warriors—comprising an estimated four hundred to one thousand warriors—was heading to Crow country on a raid. Or, possibly, they knew the survey party was in the area and were specifically searching for it. At about 3:00 A.M. on August 14, the warriors came upon the camp. Because soldiers had noticed some signs of Sioux in the area, 1st Lieutenant William Logan had posted twenty-six guards that night.

However, McClernand later wrote, "The night was dark and…a few Indians succeeded in passing through the picket-line unobserved…" (McClernand, p. 30).

During the evening, the alcoholic Baker and other officers played poker and got drunk. Baker took along a keg of whiskey when he finally retired to his tent.

The Sioux who slipped past the guards into camp collected six army mules tied near the commander's tent, and took some saddles for good measure. But what they really wanted was the horse and mule herd, along with the surveyors' beef cattle. Leaving the men far from help with no transportation or food supply would certainly stop their work.

As soon as they were aware of the Sioux, Captain Charles C. Rawn and Captain Lewis Thompson went to awaken Baker so that he could give orders for defense. Rousing the commander apparently was not easy, and when the captains informed Baker of the situation he angrily told them they were just cowards who were imagining things. His only order was that they not wake the other soldiers.

McClernand wrote that

> Some people thought the pickets were deceived as to the presence of Indians, and that they were firing at imaginary red-skins, but a volley from the latter, together with their...yells and war-whoops[,] did away with that belief. (McClernand, p. 31)

The two captains, Lieutenant Logan, and other officers ignored Baker's orders and organized the soldiers. Each side later claimed that the other fired the first shot, but regardless the battle soon was on. Some of the Indians moved into the nearby trees, and others spread out for a mile atop the bluffs above the camp. Still more hid in the south end of camp, but two companies of soldiers took advantage of the darkness to move into position to surprise and attack them at dawn.

When daylight came, the Indians on the bluffs fired down into the camp. Others, including Crazy Horse, attacked by charging in circles. As the soldiers defended themselves, one sergeant was killed, and three civilians were severely wounded (one mortally). The Indians said they lost eleven dead (McClernand, p. 32).

The fight continued until mid-morning, when Sitting Bull called a halt, saying the battle had gone on long enough. Crazy Horse made one last charge, but his war pony was shot from under him. The warriors moved away, and Baker decided not to pursue them, a decision that caused further damage to his military record. Both sides claimed victory.

The surveyors went back to work that morning, but McClernand recorded that they

> realized that the strength of the escort was not sufficient to guard the moving [wagon] trains, or the camp if established, and at the same time give proper protection to the surveyors, who frequently were strung out for two or three miles. As a result, the Chief Engineer [Thomas Rosser] three days later decided to discontinue the survey along the Yellowstone, and asked to be escorted across country to the Musselshell River, to run a line along that stream and…to the Missouri. This was done. (McClernand, pp. 32–33)

As a result of the 1872 battle, a much larger military escort accompanied surveyors during the summer of 1873. The crews planned to fill in the missing part of the Northern Pacific's route through the unceded lands. Among the 1,500 troops, 400 civilians, and 275 supply wagons commanded by General David S. Stanley were 373 men of the Seventh Cavalry under Colonel George A. Custer.

## Custer on the Yellowstone

The 1873 survey reunited Custer with another member of his West Point Class of 1861, his good friend Thomas L. Rosser. The tall, olive-complexioned Rosser had dropped out of the academy just before their graduation to join the Confederate army. Achieving the rank of general, Rosser led extensive raids in the Shenandoah Valley, destroying bridges and railroad facilities and capturing tons of U.S. Army supplies. Confederates nicknamed Rosser "The Savior of the Valley."

In 1864, General Philip Sheridan had had enough of Rosser's raids and assigned Custer to stop his old buddy. Custer's and Rosser's forces fought in October 1864 near Woodstock, Virginia. Custer's larger Union battalion routed the Confederates, chasing them down the Shenandoah Valley in what the victors jokingly called "the Woodstock Races," and capturing some of Rosser's artillery, his supply train and headquarters wagons. Historian Stephen E. Ambrose recounts how Custer, the practical joker, dressed in one of Rosser's uniforms—hilariously oversized on the smaller Custer. He even sent a note across enemy lines asking Rosser to have his uniforms tailored smaller for their next meeting (Ambrose, p. 203). Rosser's response was another skirmish a few days before Christmas, when he captured forty of Custer's men.

After the Civil War, Rosser went to work as a railroad builder and by 1873 had worked his way up to the position of chief engineer of the Northern Pacific Railroad. As a result he was assigned to the Yellowstone Expedition camp as the man in charge of getting the line built through the unceded lands. And found Custer under arrest.

General Stanley, ten years older than Custer, was a steady, not flashy, soldier—and a heavy drinker. The teetotaling Custer was his exact opposite, and soon the two loathed each other. Stanley's opinion of the junior officer was that he was "a cold-blooded, untruthful and unprincipled man. He is universally despised by all the officers of his regiment excepting his relatives and one or two sycophants" (Stewart, p. 170).

Stanley believed that Custer's insubordination meant he was trying to take over the whole command. Custer soon made the mistake of taking off on his own as the surveyors reached the Little Muddy River, near today's Williston, North Dakota. Fifteen miles away from Stanley, Custer sent him a note asking for a delivery of rations and forage—just when Stanley had planned to have Custer supervise getting the command across the Little Muddy.

Stanley not only arrested Custer, he also deviated from standard army practice and moved the Seventh Cavalry to the end of the line of march, where the troops rode in the dust cloud created by the marching infantry. Chief Engineer Rosser, arriving at the camp and finding Custer confined to a tent, immediately let Stanley know that the railroad company would not be pleased with this punishment. Stanley returned Custer to the head of the Seventh, and the Seventh to the head of the line. Custer in turn treated his commander with proper respect as the expedition continued into Montana Territory.

Generally, Custer's job was to take a small command forward to decide the best route for the expedition wagons, at which he was very skilled. On August 4, 1873, he and eighty-five men traveled upstream on the north side of the Yellowstone River and halted opposite the mouth of the Tongue River, and opposite today's Miles City. Except for a few men on guard, the relative handful of soldiers were relaxing—Custer himself napping with his boots off and horse unsaddled—when 350 Sioux and Northern Cheyenne warriors under Crazy Horse found them. It would be the first of three battles between Custer and Crazy Horse.

Because the Sioux and Cheyennes had few guns among them, Crazy Horse had most of his men hide in a large grove of trees upstream along the Yellowstone from the Seventh. Then he sent six men as decoys to stampede Custer's horses toward the trees. On foot and fighting in close quarters in the trees, the cavalry would be at a disadvantage.

When the decoys rode through the camp shouting and shooting, Custer chose two men to join him in following the Indians as quickly as possible and assigned twenty men to Captain Tom Custer to come behind in reserve. The decoys yelled insults and occasionally fired as they moved toward the trees—but they stayed in sight, riding back and forth. Custer sensed an ambush and halted to see what the Indians would do.

In the trees were some Southern Cheyennes who had survived Custer's November 1868 attack on their village on the Washita River in present-day Oklahoma. Because warriors from Black Kettle's village were said to have been raiding Kansas homesteads, Custer and his troops had killed men, women, and children, plus most of their nine hundred horses, in a dawn attack. Now the Cheyennes recognized "Long Hair," as they called him, and charged out of the trees to avenge their relatives. Crazy Horse's trap was ruined. The Sioux followed, but let the Cheyennes make repeated charges while they fired their own guns infrequently. The soldiers shot many of the Cheyennes who rode at them singly and in small groups.

Concerned about running out of ammunition before Stanley and the main command arrived, Custer organized a charge that scattered the Sioux and Cheyennes and drove them off. Winning this skirmish gave the colonel a deep, and ultimately deadly, belief that the Sioux and Cheyennes were "cowardly" and one good charge was all it took to beat them.

A few days later, Arikara scout Bloody Knife led Custer's troops on the war party's trail to opposite the mouth of the Bighorn River. The Indian village had crossed the Yellowstone here, but the cavalry troops wasted all day trying to figure out how to get their horses across. When the sun rose the next morning, on August 11, the Sioux and Cheyennes began firing into Custer's camp from atop the bluffs on the Yellowstone's south side. The women and children stood nearby watching.

Then Crazy Horse led two groups, each with about one hundred warriors, across the river, one upstream and one downstream from the soldiers, while others continued firing across the water. Custer responded quickly with a charge that destroyed the Indians' momentum, and the cavalry continued chasing the warriors for nine miles before the Sioux and Cheyennes recrossed the river. Four soldiers were killed and four wounded in the day's battle.

So, twice in 1873 Custer had routed Sioux and Northern Cheyennes with a single charge. The third time that he and Crazy Horse would face each other, at the Little Bighorn in 1876, Custer would try the same tactic and fail.

Railroad work in the unceded lands abruptly stopped after 1873, not because of Sioux resistance but because the United States fell into a huge economic depression, the Panic of 1873. The Northern Pacific was among companies large and small that went into bankruptcy. For the Northern Pacific, that meant no construction for two years while it reorganized. When accounts of gold in the Black Hills came from Custer's Black Hills Expedition of 1874, many Americans saw an opportunity. Jobless men rushed there, hoping for gold—even though the area was sacred to the Sioux and legally closed to whites. This antagonized both reservation-dwelling and nontreaty Sioux who believed the Black Hills had been permanently protected by the Fort Laramie Treaty of 1868.

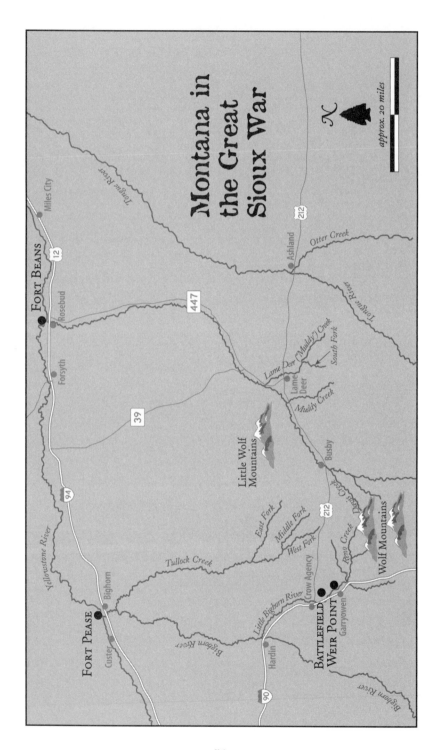

Montana in
the Great
Sioux War

N

approx. 20 miles

# THE GREAT
# SIOUX WAR BEGINS
# — 1876 —

The Great Sioux War, as today's historians call it, began during the United States' centennial year, when segments of the largest Great Plains Indian nation fought to maintain their buffalo-following life. The Sioux, Northern Cheyennes, and Arapahos won notable victories— especially along Montana's Little Bighorn River—but eventually were worn down by the U.S. Army. Soon after, the land where the Indians had traveled freely to follow the bison was surrounded by white settlers moving in from the east, the south, and the west.

When the army sent an expedition under Colonel George A. Custer into the Black Hills on the Great Sioux Reservation in July 1874, many men around the nation were desperate for jobs. The Panic of 1873 still gripped the United States. Lasting for four years, that depression put one-fourth of workers on the street, and cut farmers' incomes to nearly nothing. Expedition members published statements that the area held "gold at the grass roots"—gold that would be easy to recover (Stewart, p. 65). Their exaggerated tales, combined with the bad economy, produced an illegal stampede of prospectors into sacred Sioux land.

The Black Hills Expedition's goal had been to locate a site for a military fort to help control the nontreaty Sioux. General Philip H. Sheridan, commander of the army's Military Division of the Missouri, had ordered the 1874 trek with President Ulysses S. Grant's blessing. In September 1875 a government commission went to the Great Sioux Reservation to buy the Black Hills and unceded Sioux territory in southeastern Montana. The Sioux faced the commission and refused to sell, with both treaty and nontreaty leaders unified. However, in

November, the government gave up the pretense of evicting miners from the Black Hills (Stewart, p. 69).

According to a Lakota creation story, the first Sioux people had emerged from a dark underground world into this world of blue sky and green grass through Wind Cave in the Black Hills. When they found they could not return home, one of their leaders turned himself into a bison, the animal that supplied food, clothing, tools, toys, and shelter. The Black Hills, *Paha Sapa* in Lakota, is to the Sioux "the heart of everything that is." They did not want to part with this sacred area, and still do not, as the modern Oglala medicine man Rick Two-Dogs explained: "We have a spiritual connection to the Black Hills that can't be sold. I don't think I could face the Creator with an open heart if I ever took money for it" (Young).

U.S. public opinion was divided on how to proceed. Many citizens favored the Peace Policy and land purchase while others supported having the army seize the Black Hills. In November 1875, Grant decided on a military campaign that would round up the nontreaty Sioux tribes and force them onto the Great Sioux Reservation, while ignoring the miners. Attempts to purchase the land would continue.

That plan, which removed the danger for Black Hills prospectors, was presented to citizens as a "peace" measure that enforced the Fort Laramie Treaty and its goals of education and pacification. John Q. Smith, Commissioner of Indian Affairs, had passed the problem of non-treaty people back to the army. The government even claimed that the decision was made partially to protect reservation Indians from non-treaty Indians!

Indian agents on the Great Sioux Reservation and at other agencies serving Sioux people were notified to send word to nontreaty bands that they must come in by January 31, 1876, or expect soldiers. By the time the order made its way through channels and to the agents, the date was December 22. Agents also were told to stop weapon and ammunition sales on reservations, even though annuities were running low that year, and reservation residents needed to hunt to supplement them. (Civilian control of annuities had become just as corrupt as the previous system, with many agents selling government-supplied food and goods to their own charges or other people.) Some treaty Indians had left the Sioux reservation and joined the nontreaty people just to be able to eat.

The Minnecoujou Sioux received word of the order just when they had begun entering the Crow Indian Reservation to attack the new trading post, Fort Pease, located where the Bighorn River joined the Yellowstone River. The Oglala Sioux village of Crazy Horse, instead of moving toward the reservation, moved away and into Montana's Powder River country. A master warrior in his mid-thirties, the eccentric and often antisocial Crazy Horse was a war leader who heartened other warriors and set a powerful example at the most important battles ahead. Like Sitting Bull, Crazy Horse avoided whites and their culture—even to the extent that he never allowed his photograph taken nor his portrait painted.

Chief Sitting Bull's village of five hundred lodges stayed on the Yellowstone River some miles to Crazy Horse's north. The forty-six-year-old Sitting Bull was a spiritual and tribal leader who taught total avoidance of almost all white people and most trade goods—especially whiskey—that whites supplied. He would be in the village that sent warriors to the Battle of Rosebud Creek, and at the Battle of the Little Bighorn, supporting Indian fighters with his strong opinions and powerful words.

Members of the smaller Northern Cheyenne and Arapaho nations also remained in the creek and river valleys of southeastern Montana, soon to be drawn into the army's 1876 campaign.

## Winter Campaign, 1876

Early in February 1876, the War Department approved General Sheridan's campaign plan, which was to begin with surprise attacks on Indian villages during late winter. As soon as General Alfred Terry received the news at his Department of Dakota headquarters in St. Paul, Minnesota, he tried to warn Sheridan what a winter campaign on the High Plains meant. Yes, the Indians would not be moving about, but for the same reasons that troops would not be able to move well. Blizzards left deep snows that high winds arranged into even deeper drifts. Steamboats could not travel on frozen rivers, and the Northern Pacific Railroad reached only to Bismarck, Dakota Territory. From the railhead, overland wagon trains had to supply troops in the field. Setting a pattern for upper-level officers throughout the war to come, Sheridan ignored this unwelcome information about conditions in land unfamiliar to him.

The campaign was to be mounted by troops in two of the five departments in the U.S. Army's Division of the Missouri, commanded by Lieutenant General Philip H. Sheridan from Chicago. Sheridan answered directly to General of the Army William Tecumseh Sherman in Washington, D.C. Within the Division of the Missouri, Sherman would use troops of the Department of Dakota, commanded by Brigadier General Alfred H. Terry. From headquarters in St. Paul, Minnesota, Terry commanded all the troops in that state and Montana and Dakota territories.

The year of 1876 found five companies of the Seventh Cavalry (A, C, D, F, and I) at Fort Abraham Lincoln, across the Missouri River from today's Bismarck, North Dakota. Under General Terry, they would be joined by the rest of the Seventh. Companies E and L had to come from Fort Totten (North Dakota), with H and M heading to "Fort A. Lincoln" from Fort Rice (South Dakota), and B, G, and K leaving detached service in Louisiana. The last three companies were among the U.S. forces occupying the former Confederacy following the Civil War as part of Reconstruction. That effort was winding down towards abandonment the following year, so the three Seventh Cavalry companies were released early to join the army campaign on the plains.

Sheridan also turned to his Department of the Platte, calling on Brigadier General George Crook, whose extensive experience as an Indian fighter had been against tribes of the Southwest and the Oregon country. Based in Omaha, Crook commanded troops stationed in the states of Iowa and Nebraska, and in Wyoming, Utah, and part of Idaho territories.

Generals Terry and Crook would take the field with their respective troops during the coming campaign.

Sherman, Sheridan, Terry, and Crook—and almost all other participating U.S. Army officers—were convinced of one thing: The nontreaty Sioux and Northern Cheyennes would elude troops rather than stand and fight. The Indians might go back to the Great Sioux Reservation in small groups, or they would cross the "medicine line," the U.S.–Canada border, where U.S. soldiers could not follow. The Indians had to be stopped from escaping.

From the beginning, the generals planned to move three independent units to surround the Indians, harass them, destroy their supplies and take their horses, prevent them from going to Canada, and force them onto the reservation. In this book the units are titled for the territories from which they set out, in the order they took to the field: the Montana Column, the Wyoming Column, and the Dakota Column.

The regiments in the Montana Column would form a northern boundary along the Yellowstone River, while the Dakota Column moved in from the east and the Wyoming Column from the south. While the columns would try to coordinate their efforts, they were never meant to meet at a single place on a given day. Historian Edgar I. Stewart states that they "were expected to rendezvous at a common center, probably somewhere on the Big Horn or Little Big Horn rivers" (Stewart, p. 82). They were to surround the nontreaty people in southeastern Montana, where Indian agents had reported that those particular Sioux and Cheyennes wintered.

As Gen. Sheridan wrote to General of the Army Sherman at the end of May:

> *...I have given no instructions to Generals Crook or Terry, preferring that they should do the best they can under the circumstances and under what they may develop...I presume the following will occur: General Terry will drive the Indians [from the east] toward the Big Horn valley, and General Crook will drive them back toward Terry, Colonel Gibbon moving down on the north side of the Yellowstone to intercept...*

any Indians trying to cross it and go north to the Missouri River. Some of Sheridan's confidence in the campaign came from his mistaken belief that "hostile Indians in any great numbers can not [sic] keep the field as a body for a week, or at most ten days..." (Stewart, p. 219).

General George Crook headed the Wyoming Column leaving Fort Fetterman, composed of ten troops of the Second and Third Cavalry and two companies of the Fourth Infantry, plus an eighty-six-wagon supply train carrying forage for the horses and a four hundred-mule pack train. Their assigned destination was the Powder River country in Montana.

Colonel George Custer originally was to head the Dakota Column leaving Fort Abraham Lincoln, made up of twelve companies of the ten-year-old Seventh Cavalry that he commanded, plus two companies of the Seventh Infantry, one of the Sixth Infantry, a company from the Twentieth Infantry with three Gatling machine guns, the regimental band, 150 military and civilian supply wagons wrangled by nearly two hundred men, and a beef herd for slaughter in the field. However, because of Custer's past misbehavior and and his Congressional testimony, Terry was required to replace him as Dakota Column leader, but sought permission to allow Custer to ride at the head of the Seventh Cavalry itself. (While General Sheridan was pro-Custer, General Sherman and President Grant were very much not. Having Terry command the Dakota Column but letting Custer lead only the Seventh was their compromise.)

General Sheridan was well known for favoring winter battles, when Indian hunters' food supplies were low and hunting was sparse. In summer, Plains Indian tipi villages could be packed and moved quickly, which winter weather prevented. Sheridan wanted the three columns to be in the field by March 1876, which would be deeper winter on the southeastern Montana plains than he realized. Only the Wyoming Column and part of the Montana Column were able to meet this deadline.

At the end of February 1876, Colonel John Gibbon received orders from Terry to collect all the soldiers he could spare from his four Montana garrisons and march them to Fort Ellis, three miles east of Bozeman. As commander of the District of Montana, Gibbon led the headquarters and six other companies of the Seventh Infantry at Fort Shaw, two more companies at Camp Baker on the Smith River, and another at Fort Benton on the Missouri. Fort Ellis, also under Gibbon's command, was garrisoned by two companies of the Seventh Infantry and four of the Second Cavalry.

Gibbon, who had survived his Civil War service with a good record and a severe limp, was a dependable commander. He left Fort Shaw on March 17 with five companies of the Seventh Infantry totaling twelve officers and two hundred men, carrying rations for ten days. Ten supply wagons accompanied them as they marched through deep snow in sub-zero temperatures. Frostbite and snow blindness were frequent companions on the 180-mile, eleven-day trek. Captain Walter Clifford, in charge of Camp Baker, left that west-central Montana post with one more company of the Seventh Infantry when weather permitted on March 14, and reached Fort Ellis on March 22.

## Relieving Fort Pease

Only eight days after Terry and Crook received formal notice of a winter campaign to begin in March, trader Paul W. McCormick struggled into Fort Ellis on February 18, asking the army for help. Minnecoujou Sioux had been attacking the trading post, Fort Pease, that he, partner Fellows D. Pease, and others including George Herendeen and Mitch Boyer had built the previous June. They had sited it at what promised

to become a prime location, the mouth of the Bighorn River on the Yellowstone River. Business would be good at the Crow Reservation site, they believed, when General Sheridan built his intended two military forts on the Yellowstone. Of Fort Pease's forty-six resident traders and trappers, six had been killed and eighteen wounded after seven months of Sioux attacks. McCormick had to sneak out during a blizzard and trudge through snow for four days to seek aid.

*General James Brisbin. No date, photographer unidentified.* COURTESY MONTANA HISTORICAL SOCIETY.

With permission secured from General Terry, Fort Ellis commander Major James Brisbin headed out with 2nd Lieutenant Charles B. Schofield, one company of the Seventh Infantry, and four companies of the Second Cavalry. They reached Fort Pease on March 4 and discovered that by then all but nineteen of the men at the fort had slipped away under the cover of darkness. Although one of the traders had burned down a building, the entire fort had not caught fire—a boon to other troops later in 1876.

Brisbin's soldiers returned to Fort Ellis on March 17, having seen no Sioux during their 398-mile round-trip. That same day, Colonel Gibbon's infantry—the bulk of the Montana Column—started moving from Fort Shaw, while General Crook's Wyoming Column fought the Battle of Powder River, the first army defeat in the Great Sioux War.

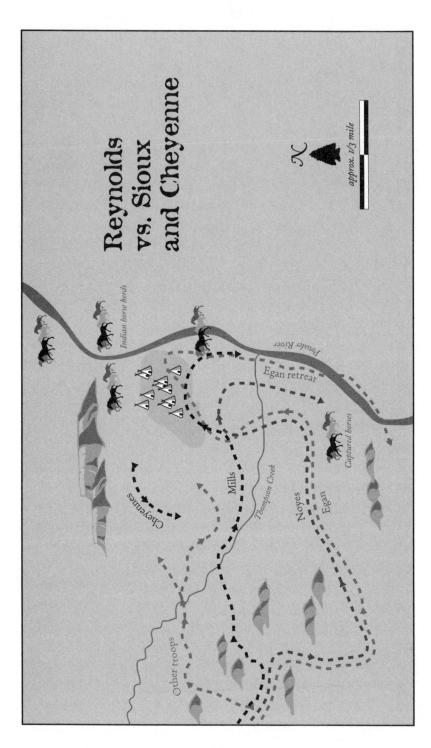

Reynolds
vs. Sioux
and Cheyenne

approx. 1/3 mile

Indian horse herds

Powder River

Egan retreat

Captured horses

Cheyennes

Mills

Thompson Creek

Noyes

Egan

Other troops

60

# BATTLE OF
# POWDER RIVER
# — 1876 —

The one and only battle of General Philip H. Sheridan's planned winter campaign in 1876 was fought on March 17 near Moorhead in extreme southeastern Montana's unceded lands. Although the army inflicted severe damage on a Sioux and Cheyenne village in the Battle of Powder River, the troops did not win and retreated hastily. Although losses were high, the Cheyennes were neither annihilated nor conquered. Nontreaty Indians were left with the sense that they could succeed in fighting off soldiers and continue to live off the reservations in the unceded lands.

Leading the Wyoming Column in this battle was the officer with the most Indian-fighting experience among all the army's Great Sioux War commanders: General George Crook. That experience, though, had been elsewhere and not against Northern Plains Indians—leaving Crook little better off than Terry, Custer, and Gibbon in this campaign.

Crook had graduated near the bottom of his West Point Class of 1852 before assignment to fight Indians in the Pacific Northwest. He fought with distinction in the Civil War, becoming one of General Philip Sheridan's most trusted officers in the Shenandoah Valley and the Richmond campaign. After the war, Crook traveled to the desert side of Oregon to fight the Paiute Indians before being appointed to command the army's Department of Arizona in 1871. His success in driving the Apaches onto reservations led to his commanding the Department of the Platte four years later.

Crook was an active leader in the field, where he dressed comfortably in a private's uniform, knew how to live off the land, used local Indians as scouts, preferred negotiating to fighting, and showed more respect for native people than did most army officers. The Sioux chief Red Cloud, foe and friend at different times, said Crook never lied to them.

## Starting from Fort Fetterman

As soon as the War Department approved the 1876 campaign plan, Crook left his Omaha headquarters and went by train to Cheyenne, Wyoming, arriving on February 18. According to Crook's loyal aide, 2nd Lieutenant John Gregory Bourke, the frontier village was aflame with Black Hills gold fever. Army quartermasters were having trouble obtaining horses because prospectors (including some army deserters) would pay any price for mounts.

Crook and Bourke reached their staging point of Fort Fetterman on the Platte River, near today's Douglas, Wyoming, on February 27, and found the fort overcrowded with troops gathering there. The Wyoming Column headed north on the former Bozeman Trail only three days later, March 1 in that leap year. Then labeled the "Powder River Expedition," the force was heading to southeastern Montana to act as the western arm pushing Indians toward General Terry's Dakota Column. No one yet knew that harsh winter weather would keep the Dakota Column at Fort Abraham Lincoln for more than another two months.

Crook may have hoped he would reach Crazy Horse's Oglala village or Sitting Bull's Hunkpapa village before the Dakota Column did. Those two Sioux men, known for their respective fighting and leadership skills, were important targets for the army. Both rejected white men's ways and refused to sign any treaties. Sitting Bull had scorned reservation Indians eight years before, telling them, "You are fools to make yourselves slaves to a piece of fat bacon, some hard-tack, and a little sugar and coffee" (Brown, p. 229).

Even though they refused to live on reservations and receive food annuities, both leaders and their warriors were glad to trade with white men and other Indian nations for guns and ammunition. Traders paid for buffalo hides and furs in older guns, so Sioux and Cheyenne warriors fought with a mixture of ten-year-old .44 caliber Winchester repeating rifles, Henry rifles, Sharps military-issue rifles, muzzleloaders, and carbines (the shorter-barreled rifle that cavalry troops used). Even so, many warriors still did not own guns, and used bows, arrows, lances, and war clubs in battle. Wooden Leg, then a sixteen-year-old Cheyenne warrior, explained that

*Bows and arrows were in use much more than guns. An Indian using a gun had to jump up and expose himself long enough to shoot. From their hiding places, Indians could shoot arrows in a high and long curve, to fall upon the soldiers or their horses. (Viola, p. 57)*

U.S. Army cavalry units carried their own forage for their horses so that natural grazing conditions would not dictate their routes. With that burden of supply wagons, the Wyoming Column extended for two miles across the snowy ground as it left Fort Fetterman. Ten companies from the Second and Third Cavalry followed thirty-one civilian scouts, with two companies of the Fourth Infantry behind the horsemen. Five ambulances, eighty supply wagons, and one hundred pack mules followed, and behind them ambled a forty-five-head beef herd that was food on the hoof.

The scouts, who were essential to the operation, were commanded by Major Thaddeus Stanton and included twenty-six-year-old Frank Grouard, a hulking man who claimed to be the son of a Mormon missionary and a Polynesian woman and said he had run away from home after his family moved from the South Seas to the United States. In reality, he had been born of the union of a French Creole man and an Oglala woman. But he had lived in both Sitting Bull's and Crazy Horse's villages before an unexplained feud with the Sioux, who he claimed were offering a reward for his death. Grouard therefore knew the favorite wintering places of these nontreaty Sioux and was familiar with the trails they traveled in their annual cycle.

The Third Cavalry was under Colonel Joseph J. Reynolds, commander of their post at Fort D. A. Russell near Cheyenne, Wyoming. A West Point graduate in 1843, he had had a more varied career than the officers around him. Reynolds had returned to the military academy as a professor after three years of field service and stayed until 1855. Then he taught mechanical engineering for five years at

Washington University in St. Louis. He entered Civil War service commanding an Indiana volunteer unit and was brevetted a general at Chickamauga and again at Missionary Ridge. Reynolds rejoined the regular army in 1866 and had been commander of the Third Cavalry since 1870. Another member of the Third Cavalry was his son, 1st Lieutenant Bainbridge Reynolds.

On the second night out, only thirty-two miles from Fort Fetterman, Indians drove off the command's cattle. On the fourth night, with the troops camped by the remains of Fort Reno (named for Civil War general Jesse L. Reno, not Major Marcus A. Reno of the Seventh Cavalry), Indians eluded sentries, fired on the camp, and tried but failed to stampede the horses and mules. Crook's scouts, sent out earlier to reconnoiter and return by midnight, could only watch the rifle fire from a distance.

After starting the march the following day, General Crook decided to shorten his caravan. He sent the infantry and the wagon train back to wait at Fort Reno, after ordering cavalry troopers to pack two blankets or one buffalo robe apiece and a single piece of tent material for each two men, along with one hundred rounds of ammunition. The pack train carried another one hundred rounds per man and fifteen days' rations. The only meat the men now would have until they reconnected with the supply wagons was bacon, or any winter-lean bison that they could shoot.

That night, March 7, the cavalry marched by moonlight to Lodgepole Creek's headwaters east of abandoned Fort Phil Kearny, where they slept on frozen ground until 8:00 A.M. By dawn the clear weather suddenly ended, with a blizzard dropping snow five and six inches deep. Lieutenant Bourke wrote that the "pelting... snow...blew in our teeth whichever way we turned..." (Brown, p. 243). Clear skies four days later brought extreme cold, with the mercury in the cavalry thermometers dropping near their lowest mark at minus twenty-five degrees Fahrenheit. Experienced soldiers taught the greenhorns to warm their spoons in the fire before touching them to their lips—after breaking off the icicles hanging from their mustaches and beards.

## Into Montana

In that subzero cold, Crook and his men followed Prairie Dog Creek northwest past today's Sheridan, Wyoming, crossed into Montana, and reached the Tongue River on March 11. Scout Frank Grouard, based on his personal experience, insisted that the Indians now would be on the Powder River rather than the Tongue. Scout Louis Richard was just as certain the nontreaty bands would be on the Little Bighorn. As would happen so many times during 1876, the military commander overruled his native scouts. Crook decided to look farther down the Tongue River and sent the scouts ahead. Later, between today's towns of Birney and Ashland, Crook agreed to head southeast toward the Powder River.

At last, on March 16, Grouard saw two Indians hunting near Otter Creek. He knew they were using an established trail and that their village would be a day's march east on the Powder. Crook decided that a forced night march and dawn attack would be best, now that his men had used nine days' worth of their fifteen-day rations. They could attack, destroy the village, and return to the supply wagons in time. The Indians, Crook believed, would promptly head for the Great Sioux Reservation.

Despite usually being an active field leader, Crook this time assigned the duty to Colonel Reynolds, who would lead six cavalry companies that contained 374 men. Grouard would guide. General Crook and the remaining troopers would bring the pack train up Otter Creek to the Powder. The general later reported that he ordered Reynolds to capture and hold the village until he arrived.

With less than an hour and a half until sundown on March 16, Reynolds's command started out at 5:00 P.M. Soon they were riding through falling snow that blacked out any starlight and the moon when it rose later that night. Walking ahead of the horsemen, Grouard sometimes struggled to see the trail but managed to keep to it through twelve hours of darkness. When the men reached a hilltop above the Powder River at 4:00 A.M., Reynolds ordered a halt and sent Grouard and other scouts ahead to locate the expected village. The troopers, forbidden to build fires, huddled and shivered and struggled to stay awake until Grouard returned two hours later. The trail ahead, he said, had been recently used by a village, which had to be nearby—no doubt somewhere on the banks of the Powder River. He immediately left again to locate the village precisely.

When dawn broke at nearly 6:30 on March 17, the men had no idea that Crazy Horse's village then was a little more than thirty statute miles east, and Sitting Bull's about forty miles farther northeast near Chalk Buttes and the site of present-day Ekalaka. The village they were preparing to attack was probably that of the Cheyenne chief Old Bull, but some troopers—and a reporter present—were convinced it was Crazy Horse's. Even scout Grouard claimed that it was, when he recognized Oglala and Minneconjou horse tack, but the animals belonged to some fifty visitors.

Grouard returned after spotting the village and described how it was situated. About one hundred lodges sat on the west side of the Powder, below some bluffs. The village had seemed unguarded and still asleep when he left his vantage point. (A village this size would hold around 200 warriors, against Reynolds's 375 troops.) Reynolds and Captain Alexander Moore quickly outlined a battle plan that assigned Moore's battalion to lay down supporting fire from atop the bluffs. Captain Henry E. Noyes's troops would approach along the Powder from south of the village, driving the Indians' horse herd away to the north. Captain James Egan's men would charge the lodges to start the battle, with Captain Anson Mills's troops following to support them.

Getting the tired horses down the rocky mountainside took long enough that the intended dawn battle did not begin until after 9:00 A.M., in bright but frigid daylight. Still, the cavalry managed a surprise attack.

But Moore's intended sharpshooters could not get up their assigned bluffs in time. Egan's charge awoke the village, and the Cheyenne warriors saw their horse herd being taken while they fired back and women and children rushed to safety beyond the lodges. Cheyennes gained the bluffs before Moore could, and so there was no cavalry fire from above.

## Cheyenne Defense

Mills waited almost too long before taking his troops in among the lodges behind Egan's, who were by then off their horses and defending themselves rather than attacking—the weakest position cavalry troops could be in. Rather than fleeing as expected, these Cheyennes were standing and fighting, even trying to counterattack. Within half an hour, the Cheyennes had been pushed out of the village but continued to fire into it. The dismounted cavalry formed a skirmish line to hold the village.

To the cavalry's surprise, the lodges were well stocked with ammunition. Hit by bullets, these caches exploded and set the lodges afire (Brown, p. 98). Soldiers combined defensive fighting with ripping down and torching the village—burning lodges, fresh and preserved food, ammunition and weapons, clothing, bison robes, and cottonwood bark harvested for horses' winter forage.

Noyes, having captured the Cheyenne horses (estimates range from six hundred to one thousand head) and driven them away, believed the battle was over for his men. He allowed most of his men to begin making coffee and unsaddle their horses to graze. Later explaining this decision, Noyes summarized the trying situation:

> The horses had been under the saddle for twenty-six hours and had had no forage since the camp at Otter Creek. The men had ridden fifty-five miles without rest since early the morning of the day before and had not eaten since the previous evening. (Vaughn, Reynolds Campaign, p. 111)

But when the Cheyennes fought back, Reynolds urgently summoned Noyes and his men to join the skirmish line—on foot if necessary. Noyes left nineteen men to guard the captured horse herd and returned with fifty-one troops.

Reynolds ordered his command to withdraw under fire at about 1:30 P.M. and, as they backed away from the ruins, forty or more Cheyenne warriors entered from the other side. Four dead soldiers were left on the field unburied, and five or six wounded were pulled away by travois. Leaving their dead comrades to expected mutilation by the Cheyennes angered the soldiers, and lowered both their morale and the Third Cavalry's reputation within the army. Lieutenant Bainbridge Reynolds would spend the rest of his life trying to defend his father's decision and honor.

Colonel Reynolds, immediately concerned about the safety of the his survivors, ordered another forced march, and the cavalry and the Cheyenne horse herd retreated twenty miles by nightfall. After crossing back into Wyoming, they camped at the mouth of Clear Creek on the Powder River. Reynolds assigned no one to guard the captured horses, and the exhausted, hungry soldiers fell deeply into their first sleep in thirty-six hours.

But the Cheyennes did not sleep that night. Despite Grouard's prediction it would not happen, some warriors caught up with the cavalry by dawn on March 18 and recaptured all but one hundred of their horses. Meanwhile, the Cheyenne women and children began moving east toward Crazy Horse's village, leaving blood on the snow in the subfreezing night that saw the deaths of several noncombatants. They took three days to reach safety in the Oglala village, where news of the attack fed the Indians' determination to stand up to the army. The Sioux village was too small to help the Cheyennes, and so the combined villages decided to go on to join Sitting Bull's people near Chalk Buttes.

Reynolds refused to let his men go after the horses that were seen vanishing in the distance on March 18. As he later stated, "The limit of human endurance had been reached. We were all, men and horses, completely worn out" (Vaughn, *Reynolds Campaign*, p. 140). The men had no food left and were stiff from riding, then fighting, then sleeping on bare ground. Reynolds sent his scouts to locate General Crook (and a little food), but by 2:00 P.M. he was ready to start moving back to Fort Reno without him—just as Crook and his men came into view.

As soon as the Wyoming Column reunited, they began the seventy-mile trek to their supply wagons at Fort Reno, which they reached on March 20. By then all the forage was gone, and fifty-eight horses and thirty-two mules had been killed or abandoned because of exhaustion. Crook allowed the men and animals to rest a day when thawing temperatures turned the Bozeman Trail to mud. The command finally arrived at Fort Fetterman on March 26.

What the army's expedition had accomplished was to combine three villages into a larger one filled with angry people. Crook brought charges against Reynolds, Noyes, and Moore for "misbehavior before the enemy" by not holding the village and the captured horses, and abandoning him in the field on the assumption that the Cheyennes had attacked and beaten Crook's troops. He also charged Captain Moore with "cowardice." As charges and countercharges flew during the men's courts-martial that following year, many army officers and enlisted men developed either pro-Crook or pro-Reynolds opinions. These would color their attitudes towards each other for years to come. Reynolds and Moore were convicted of "misbehavior," but President Ulysses S. Grant set aside their sentences. Noyes was simply given a reprimand. Reynolds subsequently retired from the army.

Upon receiving Crook's first report of this battle, General Philip Sheridan wired back that Crook and his men should return to the field as soon as the horses were rested. But soon enough Sheridan learned how impossible a winter campaign was in that corner of Montana, Dakota, and Wyoming. General of the Army William T. Sherman found the Powder River battle "not conclusive or satisfactory" (Brown, p. 159). The Northern Cheyennes consider this a minor battle in their history, and later said that only one warrior had died in the fighting, while some women and children died during their march through the snow. At Fort Fetterman, the Sioux chief Spotted Tail told a member of Crook's staff: "If you don't do better than you did the last time, you had better put on squaws' clothes and stay at home" (Brown, p. 249).

By the end of March, General George Crook had returned to Omaha, where he would stay for two months. He had informed General Sheridan that the Wyoming Column could not take the field again until mid-May at the earliest. The Dakota Column was still snowbound at Fort Abraham Lincoln. Only the Montana Column was moving into the field, breaking through deep snow along the Yellowstone River, alone and traveling farther and farther from supporting forces.

## Montana Column on the Move

After its freezing march from Fort Shaw to Fort Ellis in Montana Territory (during the time of the Wyoming Column's movement and defeat), the Montana Column rested for only two days. It left Fort Ellis on March 30, moving toward expected cooperation with Crook's Wyoming Column.

Its orders were to go to the Yellowstone River and then south on the Bozeman Trail to abandoned Fort C. F. Smith (near today's Yellowtail Dam on the Bighorn River). From there, they would search the valleys of the Little Bighorn River, Rosebud Creek, and the Tongue River, trying to locate and attack any nontreaty Indians. Lieutenant James H. Bradley was in command of twelve mounted scouts, and he would hire twenty-five more Crow scouts early in April. Among them were the teenaged Curley and the outstanding Sioux and French scout Minton "Mitch" Boyer, who had been trained by Jim Bridger.

Thirteen officers and 220 men in six infantry companies now comprised the Montana Column, which also transported two Gatling guns and a Model 1857 12-pounder field gun, nicknamed the "Napoleon," that shot spherical explosive shells. On April 1, Gibbon and Brisbin—along with ten officers, army surgeon Dr. Holmes O. Paulding, and 185 men in Companies F, G, H, and L of the Second Cavalry—left Fort Ellis to join the infantry.

Heavy snows made for slow going, with only sixteen to nineteen miles' progress each day. April 8 found the men camped on the Yellowstone River at the site of present-day Columbus. Now orders arrived from General Terry (sent by telegraph and courier from his St. Paul headquarters to Fort Ellis and then into the field) canceling their move to Fort C. F. Smith. These orders were the result of General Crook's and Colonel J. J. Reynolds's Battle of Powder River. Now the Montana Column was to begin patrolling the north side of the Yellowstone River and especially watching the major ford at the Rosebud's mouth, east of today's Forsyth.

Moving east, downstream along the Yellowstone, with Bradley's scouts leading the way, the Montana Column passed Pompeys Pillar on the warm spring afternoon of April 17. Four days later, they received new orders sent from General Terry on April 15. The Dakota Column was still stuck at Fort Abraham Lincoln because of spring snowdrifts on the prairie. The Wyoming Column was back at its Fort Fetterman field camp after its March expedition to the Powder River. Both Crook and Custer believed they could not move out for another month. General Sheridan's misguided plan for a winter campaign was truly dead.

*Gatling gun battery, Fort Lincoln, D.T. 1877. Photograph by F. Jay Haynes.*
HAYNES FOUNDATION COLLECTION, MONTANA HISTORICAL SOCIETY.

Gibbon and his men were already far into the unceded lands of nontreaty Indians, more than two hundred miles from Fort Ellis, with no chance of reinforcements. Terry, therefore, ordered the Montana Column to hole up in the abandoned Fort Pease. At this point, the infantrymen who left Fort Shaw with Gibbon on March 17 had marched nearly four hundred miles. They retraced their path along the Yellowstone and began to settle in at Fort Pease, building platforms for beds and setting up bowers to protect their tents. The men hunted and fished daily for recreation and to extend their rations.

Captain Edward Ball, with some white and Crow scouts and two cavalry companies, left the main group and took a different route to Fort Pease, traveling south up the Bighorn River as far as Fort Smith. Then they moved east to the upper Little Bighorn and scouted it downstream. Finally, they followed Tullock Creek downstream (northwest) to the Bighorn near its mouth at today's town of Bighorn. This loop put them on the west bank of the Little Bighorn for a noon rest near the end of April, almost at the exact spot where the great Lakota and Northern Cheyenne village would stand two months later. There the Crow scout

Jack Rabbit Bull marked an empty box with pictographs that, he explained, told the Sioux just what the soldiers planned to do to them. Captain Ball and his men reported seeing no Indians during their circuit.

But the Indians were aware of the soldiers in the area. On the night of May 2–3, during a heavy dust storm at Fort Pease, fifty Cheyennes led by Two Moon captured a picketed horse and mule belonging to Fort Shaw guide Henry Bostwick, and all but seventeen of the Crow scouts' free-roaming ponies. (Although the Crows would capture a few Sioux horses, they would return to the Crow Reservation later in May to replace their mounts.)

On May 3, couriers who arrived with mail from Fort Ellis reported being shot at, about ten miles from Fort Pease.

Four days later, Lieutenant Bradley talked a reluctant Colonel Gibbon into allowing him to lead the scouts out to investigate whether the horsetakers came from a nearby village, as Bradley believed. Wanting to keep their own presence secret, Bradley and his men started out on a night march on May 7. After an eighty-five-mile circuit, the party returned two days later, reporting no Indians. Gibbon, convinced the nontreaty Indians were farther down the Yellowstone, ordered camp (but not all the supplies) moved to Little Porcupine Creek, fifty more miles into the field. Here, just east of today's Forsyth, the Montana Column camped from May 14 through 19, then moved east to opposite the mouth of Rosebud Creek, where they would stay until June 5.

Agents on the Great Sioux Reservation were reporting that village sites there were nearly abandoned, with many winter residents leaving for the summer hunting. General Sheridan in Chicago believed they were leaving to fight. On May 30, he wrote to General Sherman, saying that "all the agency Indians capable of taking the field are now, or will be, on the warpath..." (Stewart, p. 219).

## Bradley Finds the Village

Even without having that news, Lieutenant Bradley was still eager to locate the nontreaty Indian villages. Again with Gibbon's reluctant permission, Bradley set out with two dozen scouts on May 16, crossed the

Yellowstone, and began moving up the Rosebud. Late in the afternoon, from a hill that historian John Gray locates at the headwaters of Sweeney Creek, they saw a stationary smoke cloud about eighteen miles from the mouth of the Tongue River on the Yellowstone. Below it, they knew, was a village, its lodges hidden by bluffs. The Crow scouts estimated, from the cloud's size, that the village probably held three hundred lodges, which meant eight hundred to one thousand warriors. The scouts refused to go any nearer, and Bradley relented and returned to the Gibbon camp, arriving at dawn after marching all night.

Colonel Gibbon at first welcomed the news and quickly planned an attack that would both give his bored men and Crow scouts some action and let the Montana Column make the campaign's first strike. Leaving one company to guard the camp, he mustered thirty-four officers, 350 men, and nearly thirty scouts—to face at least twice as many Sioux and Cheyennes. They would travel light, taking seven days' rations, 150 rounds of ammunition, and one blanket per man on thirty pack mules. As they prepared, seventy-five to one hundred Sioux warriors appeared across the Yellowstone on the south side, probably having followed Bradley and the scouts' return trail. Disappointed, Gibbon believed he had just lost the chance for a surprise attack, unaware that the Indians had known of his presence since before Bradley's survey.

Despite that, Colonel Gibbon ordered his cavalry to cross the Yellowstone River, which now was swollen with spring snowmelt. During the first hour, four horses drowned and only ten troopers safely made the crossing. Those losses, along with Gibbon's belief that they had been discovered, were enough to make him cancel the foray. Some of the Crow scouts said he was simply afraid to fight the Sioux and Cheyennes.

Instead, Gibbon sent two cavalry companies under Captain Lewis Thompson to scout along the Yellowstone's north side to the mouth of the Tongue River with orders to look for any sign that the large village had moved. Couriers were expected shortly from Fort Ellis, and Gibbon sent Bradley and a few scouts in the opposite direction, upstream, to meet them. On May 19, Bradley found and escorted the couriers to base camp. Their news was that the Dakota Column under General

Alfred Terry and Colonel George Custer had at last left Fort Abraham Lincoln and could be expected to arrive in one month. Gibbon was to continue patrolling the Yellowstone's north side to contain any non-treaty Indians in southeastern Montana east of the Crow Reservation.

The next day, two Crow scouts left for the Sioux village to capture horses, but returned quickly, saying they had met a war party heading for Rosebud Creek. Gibbon immediately left to reinforce Captain Thompson. Leaving one company at camp, Gibbon led the rest of his command down the Yellowstone in a forced march during a major rainstorm. To their relief, no tracks at the mouth of the Rosebud indicated that the Indians had crossed to follow Thompson. Lieutenant Bradley took a small group farther downstream but did not find the cavalry troops, and returned thinking he and Thompson had passed each other. Thompson and his men arrived in camp safely on May 21, and described how a band of warriors had appeared on the south side of the Yellowstone, seeming ready to attack, but had given up attempting to cross after testing the raging river with poles.

Now certain that the area around the mouths of the Rosebud and the Tongue were where his troops should be, Gibbon ordered the rest of the supplies moved downstream to the Little Porcupine from Camp Supply at the mouth of the Stillwater. The contract with the civilian teamsters of the John W. Power company expired on May 23, so the cavalry had to escort those wagons back to Fort Ellis, and take the replacement E. G. Maclay & Co. wagons into the field. As the escort and the Maclay wagons headed for the main command, Sioux warriors appeared on ridges waving lances and guns. Hunting parties near the base camp were fatally fired upon on May 23. That same day, scout George Herendeen rushed in from hunting to alert Gibbon to an attack on another hunting party. The three cavalry companies who rode to the rescue were too late, finding the bodies of cavalry privates Augustus Stoker and Henry Raymeyer, as well as civilian drover James Quinn. Only Stoker had been scalped, but all three bodies had been severely mutilated. Feeling that his camp was under observation, Colonel Gibbon now ordered the Napoleon gun manned all night long, an order enforced until the command left the site on June 5.

## "We Do Not Want to Fight"

A few days later, scouts Thomas H. LeForge and Mitch Boyer spotted some Sioux warriors across the Yellowstone River. Using Plains Sign Language, the warriors messaged: "…we are now out hunting for food. Many of our women are walking because we have not enough horses, and our children are hungry. We do not want to fight the white people, and we wish the soldiers would…leave us alone.… We will stay here and kill buffalo, where they are plentiful.… Tell this to your chiefs" (Stewart, p. 153).

Gibbon's response was to send Bradley and twenty scouts across the Yellowstone on May 27 to look for Indian activity. Infantry troops under Captain Clifford, Bradley's superior, provided cover from the bluffs as the command moved toward the Little Wolf Mountains, spotting fresh bison kills and week-old pony tracks that moved from the Tongue River to Rosebud Creek. This was just as the Crow scouts had reported a week before.

Bradley returned to his vantage point above Sweeney Creek and peered through binoculars up the Rosebud Valley. Now he saw a vast village that stretched for two miles along Rosebud Creek, with many columns of smoke filling the air. Several Cheyenne lodge circles sat among those of several tribes of Sioux Indians. The village was only about eighteen miles from Gibbon's Little Porcupine base camp.

Trading boats led by former Fort Pease co-owner Paul McCormick arrived at camp on May 28, bringing orders from General Terry for Gibbon to move down the Yellowstone to Glendive Creek, cross the Yellowstone, and "cooperate" with the Dakota Column. Terry believed the nontreaty Indians had gone that far north (Glendive Creek meets the Yellowstone at today's town of Glendive), but Gibbon and Bradley knew better. Gibbon delayed following Terry's order until supply wagons arrived from Fort Ellis, and he did not begin moving down the Yellowstone until June 5.

The Wyoming Column had finally started toward Montana from Fort Fetterman on May 31, traveling in stinging high winds while the thermometer read zero. A blizzard beginning the next day piled up two-foot drifts and kept the command snowbound for two days. In Montana, the same storm kept Gibbon's command trapped inside their bowered tents for two days. The Dakota Column, moving west in North Dakota, also weathered this storm, although on June 3 the weather abruptly turned so hot that General Terry suffered sunstroke. Still, the command managed to travel twenty-five miles—their best one-day progress since leaving Fort Abraham Lincoln on May 17. That trek took them into present-day Montana on Beaver Creek southeast of Glendive, and they continued to move west toward the Yellowstone River.

With no sign of Indians at or south of the Little Missouri River in western North Dakota, Terry's "high hopes of a speedy campaign" (Stewart, p. 218) were dashed. On June 3, scouts sent by Gibbon reached Terry and the Dakota Column with information about the many Sioux and Cheyennes south of the Yellowstone and the three recent deaths in the Montana Column. Terry replied with an order that Gibbon halt temporarily where he was. While carrying the message, though, civilian scout John W. Williamson and another messenger spotted some of the Crows scouting ahead of Gibbon's command, thought they were Sioux, and quickly backtracked. For five more days, Gibbon reluctantly moved down the Yellowstone, while Terry had no idea he was still doing so.

From his Division of the Missouri headquarters, General Philip Sheridan still insisted—to General Sherman near the end of May—that the nontreaty Indians would simply return to their reservations when they understood that Crook's Wyoming Column had nine hundred men, Terry's Dakota Column had the same number, and four hundred troops patrolled the Yellowstone in Gibbon's Montana Column. Sheridan wanted to try to settle the matter and stop the annual off-reservation circuits. He also believed that each column could not only defend itself alone, but also "chastise" any Indian groups it met.

In the field, June 3 also brought Terry a dispatch from Major Orlando Moore that his three companies of the Sixth Infantry had met the steamboats *Josephine* and *Far West* after marching overland from Fort Buford on the Missouri River at the Yellowstone's mouth. These boats belonged to the Missouri River Transportation Company, which had contracted them to the army for military personnel and freight transport.

Moore's command and the boats awaited orders at Stanley's Stockade, located where Glendive Creek flows into the Yellowstone.

This remnant of the 1873 Yellowstone railroad survey was now back in service. Armed with Gibbon's and Bradley's information, Terry replied that Moore should load freight and his troops on one of the boats and take it up the Yellowstone to the mouth of the Powder River. Terry's plan was to locate and deal with any small nontreaty Indian bands that were separated from the large village until he could locate Crook's Wyoming Column. He thought that by now the Wyoming Column might be on the Powder River tributary called the Little Powder, which begins in Wyoming and joins the Powder near today's Broadus, Montana.

Moore selected the 190-foot-long *Far West*, because its design allowed it to travel in shallower water and withstand higher winds than did the *Josephine's*, and because its captain, Grant Marsh, was the only steamboat man who knew the upper Yellowstone River's tricky, sandbar-filled waters. Marsh was said, according to historian Edgar I. Stewart, to be able to "navigate the boat on heavy dew" and guide it "anyplace where there was enough water to keep [the] bottom damp" (Stewart, p. 224). *Far West* and its passengers reached the mouth of the Powder River on June 7.

*Steamer* Far West *at Cow Island, 1880. Photograph by F. Jay Haynes.*
HAYNES FOUNDATION COLLECTION, MONTANA HISTORICAL SOCIETY.

## Crook Retreats and Advances

As for the Wyoming Column, it reached the Tongue River in today's Wyoming on June 7 (well west of the Powder and even farther from the Little Powder). But a skirmish two days later with roaming Cheyenne warriors sent General Crook back to Goose Creek near present-day Sheridan. Having lost the element of surprise, Crook decided to leave his supply wagons behind and mount his infantry on mules. Taking a more westerly route, aiming for streams that fed Rosebud Creek, he again turned toward Montana on June 15. His men carried only four days' rations apiece, plus as much ammunition as possible. Crook intended that they would resupply from Terry's forces on the Yellowstone.

During that first week of June, unaware of General Terry's order to halt, Colonel Gibbon continued to lead the Montana Column down the Yellowstone toward the Powder at about twenty miles per day. Accompanying them were the contract wagons carrying one hundred thousand pounds of supplies. Captain Clifford's Seventh Infantry company plus three scouts and Major Brisbin traveled in mackinaw boats taken from Fort Pease. Misunderstanding Gibbon's order, Clifford took the boats downstream for two days instead of only one. Thus they were far ahead of the Montana Column when they met the *Far West* at the Powder River on June 8, only a few hours before General Terry and an advance party of two Seventh Cavalry companies arrived. Terry had pushed ahead of the Dakota Column to the steamboat, planning to take it to locate Colonel Gibbon and personally obtain the desperately desired word on where the nontreaty Indians were. Now Terry was simply able to send Clifford's scout George Herendeen to bring Gibbon to meet with him aboard the steamboat.

Herendeen reached Colonel John Gibbon's bivouac at midnight on June 9. Taking along Lieutenant James Bradley, some scouts, and a cavalry company, Gibbon arrived at the Powder River the next day and sat down on the *Far West* with General Alfred Terry and Colonel George Custer to plan strategy. (Unfortunately they had no recent information from General George Crook about the Wyoming Column's whereabouts.) The village that Bradley spotted on Rosebud Creek had probably already moved to fresh grazing, maybe to the Little Bighorn. Still thinking the Indian village was farther east than it actually was, General Terry assigned Major Reno to scout the Powder and Tongue rivers. Reno's poor job of doing so (described later) contributed to the army's defeat at the Battle of the Little Bighorn.

Gibbon's orders were to return to the Montana Column and keep it at the mouth of Rosebud Creek. Before departing, he lent Mitch Boyer, his best scout, to General Terry, who in turn assigned him to Reno's scouting expedition. (The better of the two translators, Tom LeForge, had just broken his collarbone while out hunting antelope and was out of service for the campaign.) Heavy rains kept Colonel Gibbon and the men with him from reaching the Montana Column until June 14.

During this time, the combined village—Sitting Bull's Hunkpapa Sioux, Crazy Horse's Oglala Sioux, Old Bull's Northern Cheyennes, and many more people who had joined the summer hunt—was on lower Rosebud Creek again. The village had moved south after Bradley saw it last, upstream on the Rosebud. While the army officers met on the *Far West*, the Sioux were holding their sacred Sun Dance, in which men pledged their own physical and spiritual suffering over four days. This year, holy man and chief Sitting Bull gave one hundred pieces of skin cut from his arms with an awl and knife. Knowing that soldiers were gathering to their north and east, as well as moving around to their south, Sitting Bull sought courage for his people as they faced army attack. The vision that came as a result of his offering showed soldiers and their Indian allies on horseback, falling into the Sioux village, he later said, "coming down like grasshoppers, head first, with their hats falling off." A voice told Sitting Bull, "I give you these because they have no ears" (Stewart, p. 195). He interpreted this message to mean an Indian victory, which encouraged everyone in the great village.

After the Sun Dance ended, around June 14, the village moved to the Little Bighorn River. Sitting Bull and the other Sun Dance participants rested in their lodges, recovering from their sacrifices. When news arrived that General Crook's troops were moving toward them down Rosebud Creek, some of the warriors left to stop the army force before it reached the village (Stewart, pp. 161, 191).

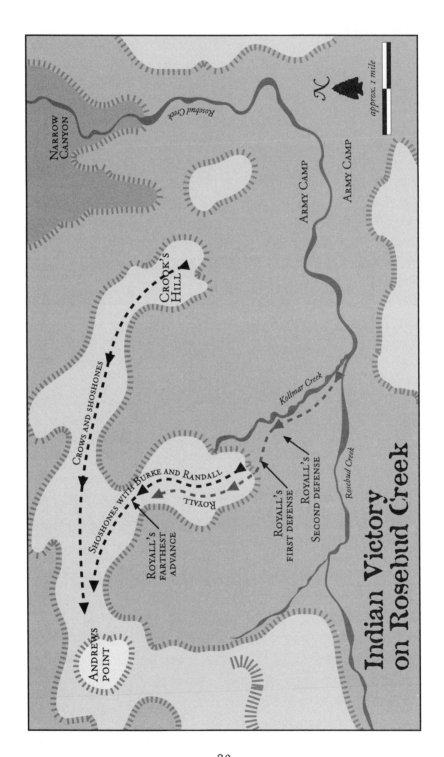

# Indian Victory on Rosebud Creek

Narrow Canyon

Rosebud Creek

Crook's Hill

Crows and Shoshones

Andrews Point

Shoshones with Burke and Randall

Royall's Farthest Advance

Royall

Kollmar Creek

Royall's First Defense

Royall's Second Defense

Army Camp

Army Camp

Rosebud Creek

N

approx. 1 mile

# BATTLE OF
# ROSEBUD CREEK
# — 1876 —

The Battle of Rosebud Creek on June 17, 1876, was a Sioux and Northern Cheyenne victory that protected the tribes' large combined village, confirmed Sitting Bull's Sun Dance vision of defeated soldiers, and gave the Indian warriors great confidence when they were attacked by Colonel George Custer's cavalry only eight days later. General George Crook's loss on Rosebud Creek would remove the Wyoming Column—more than one-third of the army troops committed to the Great Sioux War—from combat at the Little Bighorn.

After participating in the one battle of the winter campaign—on the Powder River in March 1876—the Wyoming Column was dissolved and its regiments returned to their home forts. General Crook went back to his Omaha headquarters for less than two months, then returned to Fort Fetterman in Wyoming. Some of the troops gathered there for the summer 1876 campaign were veterans of the earlier expedition into Montana. During that expedition Crook had been amazed to see what two hundred Indians at Powder River could do to nearly twice as many army troops, so this time he gathered even more troops from various forts under his command. He also vowed not to delegate leadership in the immediate battles as he had done at Powder River.

## Summer Campaign Begins

General Crook left Omaha and returned to the field in mid-May, reaching Camp Robinson, the Red Cloud Agency garrison on the Great Sioux Reservation, on May 14. Following his habit of hiring local Indians as scouts, he spent the entire next day in fruitless talks with the Oglala

Sioux. They were not interested in helping the army battle other Oglalas and the Hunkpapa Sioux, and Crook had no takers. Chief Red Cloud said diplomatically that the Sioux people who now lived on the reservation were done with war. The general then put out calls to the Crow Indians in Montana and the Shoshones in Wyoming, although his message did not reach the Crow reservation because the telegraph wire was down. He later lessened the Wyoming Column's strength temporarily while some soldiers rode to contact the Crows, but the Crows then supplied 176 scouts and warriors (Vaughn, p. 31). Eighty-six Shoshones from what is now the Wind River Reservation in Wyoming, led by Chief Washakie, also joined the Wyoming Column (Vaughn, p. 31).

After meeting with the Sioux, Crook went on to Fort Fetterman, and the Wyoming Column hit the Bozeman Trail on May 29, 1876, twelve days after the Dakota Column had left Fort Abraham Lincoln. In only two days, the pleasant spring weather disappeared and wind scoured the Wyoming plains, driving the temperature down to zero. Sleet and then snow that turned into a blizzard filled the air around the marching troops on June 1 and 2.

More than nine hundred troops in fifteen cavalry and five infantry companies and forty-seven officers shivered northward along the trail. Colonel W. B. Royall of the Third Cavalry commanded horse troops of the Second and Third, with Major Alex Chambers of the Fourth Infantry in charge of troops from the Fourth and Ninth. Five reporters went along to cover the story for newspapers in New York, Chicago, Denver, Cheyenne, and San Francisco. Until the Crows and Shoshones arrived, the Wyoming Column would have only three scouts: Frank Grouard, "Big Bat" Pourier, and Louis Richard. More than one thousand pack mules, 120 six-mule-team wagons—with about two hundred packers and teamsters—and a few ambulances stretched the column four miles long.

In the Third Cavalry was Lieutenant Bainbridge Reynolds. He was eager to remove the slur on the Third's reputation left by the Battle of Powder River even if it meant serving under General Crook, who was having his father, Colonel Joseph Reynolds, court-martialed for his actions there.

As one veteran, Henry R. Daly, recalled about the Wyoming Column's commander, "General Crook might have been taken for a Montana miner. The only part of his uniform he wore [in the field] was an old overcoat. Except in wet weather he wore moccasins, and his light bushy beard would be gathered in a series of braids" (Vaughn, *With Crook*, p. 22). Reporter Robert Strahorn noted that the general wrapped "his long blond side-whiskers" in twine, "after the manner of an Indian scalp-lock."

Although his troops thought Crook had a good sense of humor when it was displayed, Daly said he was usually "a silent man…I have seen him walk up to a cook fire, where the troops were getting their coffee, take his turn for a cup, and then walk away and sit down on the ground and blow it off and drink it without saying a word" (Vaughn, *With Crook*, p. 22). Crook's officers stated that whatever their leader was planning would not be known until he gave the order to do it.

The Wyoming Column reached Fort Reno on June 2 as the snow ended, but found no Crow allies waiting there. The three scouts told Crook how to reach Goose Creek (then often called Wild Goose Creek), a good place to bivouac west of present-day Sheridan, Wyoming, and about a nine-day march ahead. Then they cautiously left to ride through Sioux country to the Crow reservation and take their allies to Goose Creek. Leading the soldiers himself, Crook lost the way, and on June 7 camp was made near the mouth of Prairie Dog Creek on the Tongue River, right at the Wyoming-Montana line. The general and his soldiers did not know, though, that a Cheyenne hunting party including the young warrior Wooden Leg had seen them and reported their presence. Any chance of a surprise attack had been lost.

As the Wyoming Column had been moving north, the combined Oglala and Hunkpapa Sioux and Northern Cheyenne village of Crazy Horse, Sitting Bull, and Old Bull was gradually moving up Rosebud Creek when its horse herd needed new grazing land. Messengers brought the village news of soldiers arriving from the east and south as well as patrolling the Yellowstone River to the north.

Two days after Wooden Leg and his fellow hunters reported Crook's soldiers, the Cheyenne warrior Little Hawk led warriors to the

Wyoming Column's camp on the Tongue River. The warriors burst onto the bluffs across from and above the camp, where some fired down into it while others tried to stampede the horses. Two soldiers were bruised by spent bullets, and the attack was repulsed.

Crook kept his men waiting tensely on the Tongue River all the next day, then on a rainy June 11 retreated and found Goose Creek. As the scouts had promised, this site had good water and forage and was easy to defend.

## Sun Dance

In early June, the Sioux of the combined village held their Sun Dance, where Sitting Bull had the vision of victory over the army troops. The several-day rite ended about June 14, and the village moved slowly to the Little Bighorn River (Stewart, p. 195). Tribal leaders then sent more than one thousand warriors to engage the soldiers safely away from the lodges.

While the Sun Dance was underway, on June 10, General Alfred Terry was meeting with Montana Column and Dakota Column officers aboard the steamer *Far West* on the Powder River, strategizing and speculating where Crook's Wyoming Column was.

The Crow scouts arrived three days later and, a few hours after that, so did the Shoshones with Chief Washakie. Crook ordered a feast served that night and then got down to business. He assigned infantry captain George M. Randall as chief of scouts commanding the Crows and Shoshones. The general announced that at dawn on June 16 the soldiers would head out for Rosebud Canyon, everyone mounted and each carrying four days' rations, one blanket, and one hundred rounds of ammunition. They would replenish their food when they connected with the Dakota Column somewhere to the north. Only two pack mules, carrying medical supplies and basic tools, would be taken; the supply wagons and pack train were to stay at Goose Creek. The infantry troops would ride the mules, which were trained to pull wagons, and Crook gave men and beasts one day to get used to each other. Cavalry troops and some gold prospectors who had wandered in spent the day of June 15 entertained by watching the foot soldiers tame their new mounts.

When the Wyoming Column set out on June 16, some 1,300 men

strong, they marched north along the Tongue River and then turned west toward the headwaters of Rosebud Creek. They covered thirty-three miles over broken country and made camp after 7:00 P.M., rising less than eight hours later and starting off again at six o'clock the next morning. They reached Rosebud Creek about seven miles from its headwaters, near where the creek makes roughly a right-angle turn to flow north through a narrow canyon. Crook believed the large nontreaty village was north of that canyon and that he could make a surprise attack.

*Two Moon, 1878. Photograph by S. J. Morrow.*
COURTESY MONTANA HISTORICAL SOCIETY.

Flat-topped bluffs unevenly paralleled the Rosebud about a half mile to its south, with a similar row of bluffs two hundred to six hundred yards north of the stream and a level plateau beyond the latter. The creek bottom between the bluffs formed what historian J. W. Vaughn called "an amphitheater," much narrower at the west end than at the east near the Rosebud's turn. The ground was broken and rock-strewn, dotted with bushes and trees. In the amphitheater's center, what Vaughn labeled Crook's Hill rose to the bluffs, beyond which flowed Kollmar Creek.

About 8:00 A.M. on June 17, after the Wyoming Column's vanguard crossed Rosebud Creek less than a mile west of its bend, Crook allowed the men to unsaddle and graze their horses. Some troopers erected cloth-and-stick sun shelters. The dapper Lieutenant Bainbridge Reynolds brushed his uniform free of dust. The rear of the column was still arriving half an hour later when the Crow scouts, who had traveled ahead, rode in shouting "Sioux! Sioux!" Their information about a large party of warriors led Chief Washakie, wearing his warbonnet of bison horns, fur, and feathers, to warn Crook that it was pointless to fight so many enemies. Crook soon would mistakenly think that all the nontreaty Sioux were gathered here.

The Sioux and Cheyenne warriors had marched all night from their village, then stopped to paint for battle. Hunkpapa warrior Rain-in-the-Face applied his half-black, half-red paint designed to represent the sun during an eclipse. Most who knew Crazy Horse said that his medicine, or spiritual imperative, was that he did not paint his face or wear a warbonnet, but rather loosened his hair and placed a few short straws of grass in it. Instead of painting symbols on his war horse like other warriors, he rubbed streaks of dirt on it. Others have related that Crazy Horse's face paint was red with a white zigzag down the center and white dots on the sides to represent lightning and hail. Sitting Bull had come along with the warriors, even though he was recovering from his Sun Dance offering and, as a holy man, would not fight.

About two hundred Cheyenne men and at least one woman were among the thousand warriors preparing to fight, including the war chief Spotted Wolf. Calf Trail Woman, the sister of Chief Comes-in-Sight, was riding beside her husband, Black Coyote. Little Hawk led one party of Northern Cheyenne warriors, and young Two Moon (nephew of Chief Two Moon) another.

## Sioux and Northern Cheyenne Attack

The combined Sioux and Northern Cheyenne warriors attacked sooner than planned when they heard the Crow scouts' alarm, riding over the bluffs from the north and, mostly, the northwest. The attackers underestimated the number of soldiers because the end of the column was still arriving, but the unhorsed cavalry were slow to react. The army's initial response was disorganized, "every man for himself," as historian Edgar I. Stewart stated. The soldiers were firing their guns very rapidly, as if in panic.

The Shoshones who were on the left (western) side of camp immediately followed Captain Randall and, despite Washakie's pessimism, successfully fought to hold that flank. Crazy Horse led the Sioux right at the Shoshone contingent. Rain-in-the-Face later said that Shoshones were all that kept the Sioux and Cheyennes from overrunning the soldiers on their first charge.

General Crook ordered Colonel William B. Royall to charge northwest of camp beyond Crook's Hill, up Kollmar Creek (Stewart, p. 204). Royall's charge into the center of the attacking warriors put his regiment more than three miles from the army camp. Indians halted the charge, and warriors with Crazy Horse rode into two ravines west of Crook's Hill to cut Royall's men off from the main command.

*Rain-in-the-Face, approximately 1880. Photograph by L. A. Huffman.*
COURTESY MONTANA HISTORICAL SOCIETY.

For the next two hours, Royall and his men retreated and defended themselves at a second and then a third position before being able to recross Kollmar Creek and rejoin Crook. Much of the time they were nearly surrounded and subjected to constant heavy firing by the Sioux.

Among the Cheyenne fighters was the young Comes-in-Sight, who later became a chief. After he had charged back and forth many times before the soldiers, his horse was killed under him. His sister, Calf Trail Woman, who had joined the Cheyenne charges from the beginning, saw the chief unhorsed. She galloped her own horse past him, turned sharply, and rode back, pulling the animal up just long enough for Comes-in-Sight to jump on behind her. The Northern Cheyennes always called this fight, "Where the girl saved her brother."

After sending Royall out, Crook decided to mass his men for a charge up Crook's Hill, and he sent a message to Royall to return and join it. Believing that the Indian warriors were defending a village—Crazy Horse's—just north beyond these hills, the general intended to

*The Sioux charge Colonel Royall's detachment cavalry, 1876.*

push through the warriors to the lodges.

Four companies under Captain Anson Mills, with two commanded by Captain Guy V. Henry, apparently succeeded in pushing the Sioux up and off Crook's Hill, although possibly the Sioux retreat was a tactical move. While Royall fought to the west, Crook's command took the hill at about 11:00 A.M. During the fighting the general sent a second message summoning Royall, who still did not appear.

Captain Jacob F. Munson, with six sharpshooters, six other soldiers, and Crow allies, was ordered to hold the hilltop. Other Crow warriors were placed among troops on its eastern crest, and the Shoshones were assigned to a protective line at the hill's base. There a Shoshone boy was told to hold some of the warriors' horses.

South across Rosebud Creek on a bluff overlooking the army campsite, three companies of soldiers (plus the packers and the prospectors who were accidental participants) under Captain Frederick Van Vliet and Captain Charles Meinhold fired down the slope to prevent Sioux and Cheyennes from flanking the main command from the west. Van

Vliet saw Indians moving in on the Shoshone position, but he thought they were allies and let them come. They killed and scalped the young Shoshone horse-holder on the spot.

Having taken the hill, General Crook detached seven and a half cavalry companies and put Captain Mills in charge of them, assigning them to follow Rosebud Creek downstream, around its bend, and north to the supposed village. Crook promised that the main command would join after charging across the northern bluffs. Sioux and Cheyenne warriors fired on Mills's troops, following them along the Rosebud and briefly circling Crook's main command. When Mills's Crow scouts sighted the narrow canyon ahead downstream, they refused to enter what could easily conceal enemy warriors. Captain Mills did not have to deal with this, however, because Crook had again changed his mind, and Colonel Azor H. Nickerson arrived to order the horsemen back to the main command. Mills and his men turned on the pursuing Sioux, attempting to surround them, but the Indians turned back.

About the same time Mills left the hilltop, Crook's aide John Bourke (promoted to 1st Lieutenant the previous month) and chief of scouts Randall led some Shoshones on the western flank in a charge across the top of the north bluffs. They reached "Andrews Point" above the head of Kollmar Creek and looked down to discover Royall's situation. Not only were the Sioux attacking heavily, they were trying to take the beleaguered battalion's held horses while the cavalry fought on foot. The group on Andrews Point quickly pulled back to Crook's Hill, except for Bourke and bugler Elmer A. Snow. The latter was "badly shot through both arms near the elbows," Bourke wrote in his journal.

Finally, help was sent for Captain Royall's troops, with Captain Andrew Burt's and Captain T. B. Burrowes's infantry companies laying down supporting fire to cover Royall's retreat. Another Sioux charge to get Royall's horses failed under Burt's and Burrowes's bullets, and Royall's men at last joined the main command.

Late in the fighting, on the flat land of the amphitheater, Cheyenne warrior Two Moon's horse fatigued, and the young man jumped off and ran through bullets flying fast and throwing up dust around his feet. Another Cheyenne tried to ride to Two Moon's rescue, but was turned back. Two Moon thought the day might be his last. Then Young Black Bird, later called White Shield, charged his horse alongside Two Moon, who jumped on behind Young Black Bird. After they galloped away for a distance, Young Black Bird's horse began to tire from its double burden and the previous hours of fighting. Two Sioux warriors charged at it until they recognized the Cheyenne clothing and galloped away. Cheyenne warrior Contrary Belly came along leading a horse he had captured from the army's Indian allies, and Two Moon was mounted again. Soon after that, the fighting stopped.

## Called Off

When Mills's troops returned and the Wyoming Column was once again reunited, the Sioux and Cheyennes ended the battle and left the field. Four Cheyennes stayed nearby to see what the soldiers would do next. They watched the soldiers make camp below Crook's Hill that night and bury their dead the next day before breaking camp to return to Wyoming. Crook's command was back in the main camp on Goose Creek on June 19, where the general awaited supplies and reinforcements that the army promised it would send when it could. His men would stay there for more than a month; while the Montana Column was at the Little Bighorn on June 25 and 26, the Wyoming Column was awaiting reinforcements.

General Crook first reported that the Battle of Rosebud Creek had given the nontreaty warriors "a sound thrashing." A decade later, when criticized for the loss, he claimed that if the battle had gone according to his plan it would have been a victory that stopped the Sioux and Cheyennes right there. He lamented that he had never brought charges against Captains Royall and Nickerson.

Crook had lost nine soldiers and one Indian scout, with twenty-one wounded. The Sioux counted about twenty dead or mortally wounded and the Cheyennes only one.

The Sioux and Cheyenne warriors returned to their large combined village and celebrated victory. The Northern Cheyennes, still accorded the right to determine where the village moved because they were "guests," led it next to the Little Bighorn. The site was familiar to them

but not to the Sioux. All the warriors in the many lodges were confi-
dent of their ability to beat the army troops when the Dakota Column's
Colonel George Custer charged the village the following week.

# Little Bighorn Valley

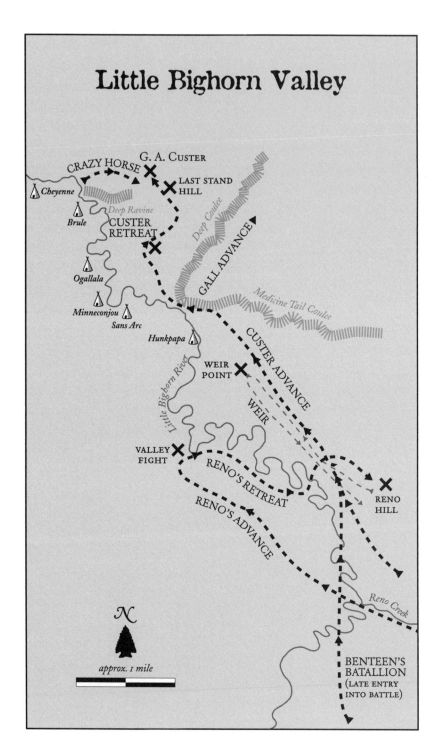

CRAZY HORSE

G. A. CUSTER

LAST STAND
HILL

Cheyenne

Deep Ravine

Deep Coulee

Brule

CUSTER
RETREAT

GALL ADVANCE

Ogallala

Medicine Tail Coulee

Minneconjou

Sans Arc

Hunkpapa

Little Bighorn River

WEIR
POINT

CUSTER ADVANCE

WEIR

VALLEY
FIGHT

RENO'S RETREAT

RENO
HILL

RENO'S ADVANCE

Reno Creek

N

approx. 1 mile

BENTEEN'S
BATALLION
(LATE ENTRY
INTO BATTLE)

# BATTLE OF
# THE LITTLE BIGHORN
# — 1876 —

The Battle of the Little Bighorn, on June 25, 1876, was not well planned or well fought by U.S. military forces. Time and again, top officers had refused to believe their hired Indian scouts about how large a force of nontreaty Sioux and Northern Cheyenne Indians seemed to be gathered at the Little Bighorn River. Furthermore, from General Alfred A. Terry to Lt. Colonel George Armstrong Custer and on down, the officers remained convinced that the Indians would pack up and move rather than stand and fight.

When the warriors of one of the largest-ever gatherings of Indians on the Great Plains did defend themselves, they completely destroyed five companies of the Seventh Cavalry and killed and wounded Indian scouts and troopers in the other companies. (Most of the men in the other seven companies of the Seventh survived that day, which popular mythology tends to forget.)

The nontreaty people were fighting for their homes, families, and way of life. But so deeply did many white people misunderstand this that Raymond Richards would write—during World War I—that the battle "was not a conflict fought desperately with the life of a nation at stake." He thus sought to compare the Battle of the Little Bighorn to the fighting in Europe of his own day. Revealing that he was thinking only of Custer's immediate command, Richards said that the battle "was a mad fight for individual lives on the part of less than 300 men—a desperate, brief struggle..." (Richards, p. 59).

News of the Battle of the Little Bighorn broke nationally during the United States' centennial anniversary, in an era of both dramatic sentimentality and commitment to Manifest Destiny, when railroad tracks and smokestacks meant progress. No trooper survived to tell exactly how events unfolded for Custer and the men he directly led. Indian participants long avoided talking to white people about their experiences for fear of punishment. During their years of silence, the story became a fertile garden where dime novelists, poets, painters, individual "sole survivors," and other profit-seeking and tribute-making whites planted many myths.

## The Personality Factor

In one brief battle, an army commander managed to get five-twelfths of his command killed and did not live to explain his decisions or battle plans. His previous career actions had caused many fellow officers and enlisted men to scorn and even hate him. Some students of the battle even suggest that other officers purposefully avoided going to the five companies' aid because they wanted him to fail. These factors, along with Indian participants' reticence, combine to demand a closer than usual look at the personalities involved in the battle.

George Armstrong Custer's better qualities were suited for reckless battlefield action, and the popular press had nicknamed him "the boy general" during the Civil War. Twice he received the temporary, or "brevet," rank of general—the first time at age twenty-three. That made him the U.S. Army's youngest general ever. He fought beside his men and did not ask them to do anything he would not, seemed tireless on long marches or low rations, and had quite a knack for "reading" the terrain of country new to him. During the war Custer impressed superiors with what historian Edgar Stewart called his "bold, reckless bravery and spectacular showmanship in several cavalry fights" (Lamar, p. 281).

But in an 1867 campaign against Cheyennes in Kansas and Nebraska, Custer pushed the Seventh's men and animals too hard, treated deserters cruelly, and once left his troops in the field while he visited Fort Riley to arrange for a supply shipment and visit his wife. He was court-martialed, convicted, and suspended from pay and rank for a year. Reinstated prematurely to fight in General Sheridan's winter 1868 campaign to force the Southern Cheyennes and Arapahos onto their

*George Armstrong Custer, approximately March 1876.*
*Photograph by Jose M. Mora.*
COURTESY MONTANA HISTORICAL SOCIETY.

Oklahoma reservation, Custer saw the chance to restore his reputation. On November 27, in a frigid dawn, he surrounded and attacked the first village he came to, killing about 140 people, including the chief and his wife. That chief, Black Kettle, had ordered both the American flag and a white flag flown over the lodges to show that the village was at peace.

Warriors from nearby villages came to fight the soldiers, and Custer quickly ordered retreat. Another group of nineteen men under Major Joel Elliott, which had taken the field two days before Custer, was missing, but faced by approaching warriors, Custer returned to base without searching for it. Elliott's command later was discovered to have been ambushed and wiped out. Indian people, army enlisted men and officers, as well as some of the public found Custer's actions disgusting. More of the public, however, remembered the "Battle of the Washita" as a victory for the army.

Custer, a lifelong practical joker, graduated last among his thirty-four West Point classmates in 1861, and with his plentiful demerits might not have made the regular army during peace time. But during the Civil War, his brashness served him well. After the war, Colonel Custer's outspokenness and love of publicity divided fellow officers into pro- and anti-Custer camps. General Philip H. Sheridan, commander of the Division of the Missouri, was a fan. When Custer did not get along with his Seventh Cavalry commander, Colonel Samuel D. Sturgis, in the late 1860s, Sheridan assigned Sturgis—a Mexican War and Civil War veteran—to detached duty as a recruiter.

Custer's command was assigned to Fort Abraham Lincoln (near today's Bismarck, North Dakota) in 1873. He was joined by his wife, and the childless couple surrounded themselves with several of his relatives. (Elizabeth Bacon Custer, called "Libbie," lived on post with her husband, and in 1876 she and Margaret Custer Calhoun even tried to go into the field aboard the steamboat *Far West*.) The Custers also selected some younger officers for their social circle, including Captain George W. Yates, 1st Lieutenant William W. Cooke, and Captain Myles W. Keogh. Outsiders sneeringly called the group "the royal family." This set filled off-duty hours with charades, dances, hunting parties complete with Custer's staghounds, and musical evenings. Present at the Little Bighorn in 1876 were brother Captain Thomas W. Custer, brother-in-law 1st Lieutenant James Calhoun, civilian brother Boston Custer, and civilian nephew Harry Armstrong Reed. Sharing the same middle name as his Uncle George, Reed also shared the same family nickname, "Autie." Tom Custer, who had come up through the ranks and held two Congressional Medals of Honor, commanded fairly universal respect from his fellow soldiers.

The 36-year-old George Custer was younger than most of his "junior" officers, and five years younger than both Captain Frederick W. Benteen and Major Marcus A. Reno. Benteen and Reno, who did not especially like each other either, composed the core of anti-Custerites in the Seventh.

Benteen was a man of principle, a Virginian who fought for the North during the Civil War even though his family disowned him for it. During the war, he briefly commanded an African-American regiment (Custer refused a similar assignment) and was a comrade-in-arms of Joel Elliott, whose death at the Battle of the Washita Benteen blamed on Custer. He had served with the Seventh Cavalry from its creation in 1866.

Marcus A. Reno was a West Pointer who had been with the Seventh since 1871 and had gone on Custer's Black Hills Expedition in 1874. When given orders, he carried them out well, but left on his own he could be indecisive on the battlefield. Reno was in charge of Fort Abraham Lincoln while Custer went to Washington, D.C., during late winter in 1876, but did not drill the men in preparation for the campaign due to start as soon as weather permitted. Before the Battle of the Little Bighorn, he had never fought Indians.

Custer's public comments during his trip to Washington, D.C.—to reporters and then a congressional investigating committee—regarding a scandal in Ulysses Grant's second administration almost kept him completely out of the 1876 campaign. Custer described how Indian agents—at that time military men—enriched themselves from annuities they were assigned to distribute to the Indian reservations. Although he was far from alone in such testimony, Custer was a soldier, and Grant, the former general, believed that no officer should speak publicly against the army. Evidence showed wrongdoing by Grant's secretary of war, William Belknap, and his own brother, Orvil. Although President Grant could do nothing about many of his accusers, he could ban Custer from the Great Sioux War. However, knowing it was a bad political move against the well-known Custer, the president compromised by banning Custer from leading the Dakota Column in the 1876 campaign. That duty went to General Terry, with Colonel Custer riding at the head of the Seventh Cavalry under Terry's command. One theory of Custer's actions at the Little Bighorn holds that he sought a spectacular victory to win back Grant's respect, or at least to show him up.

Regardless whether that was true, the colonel's previous experience fighting Sioux warriors, on August 4 and 11, 1873, at the site of present-day Miles City, had given him false confidence. He saw the cavalry as superior fighters able to overcome larger groups of fighting Sioux, or "shrieking savages," as he called them in an article published in *The Galaxy* (Custer, p. 97). As described in the chapter on Yellowstone River railroad surveyors, his small advance party, attacked by Sioux warriors on the Yellowstone River, had turned away the Indians' attack with a volley of bullets. He wrote of the August 11, 1873, fight:

> *Of course it was easy to drive them away [at first]...[As the Sioux continued to fight] [t]he effect of the rapid firing of the troopers, and their firm, determined stand, showing that they thought neither of flight nor surrender, [served] to compel the savages first to slacken their speed, then to lose their daring and confidence in the ability to trample down the little group of defenders in the front....the battle line of the warriors exhibited signs of faltering which soon degenerated into an absolute repulse. In a moment their attack was transformed into flight in which each seemed only anxious to secure his individual safety. (Custer, p. 97)*

Even as Custer was being punished for speaking freely to reporters, fate gave the colonel his own personal reporter for the 1876 campaign. For newsman Mark Kellogg, the chance meeting must have seemed a very lucky break.

When Custer and his wife were returning from Washington, D.C., to Fort Abraham Lincoln in March, they and their staghounds rode in a private car attached to a Northern Pacific Railroad train carrying army provisions and livestock from Fargo, in Dakota Territory. On the same train, heading to the Black Hills to cover the gold rush, was Kellogg. The minor newspaper correspondent met Custer and attached himself to the colonel—for what would be the greatest (and last) story of his career.

Sixty-five miles east of Bismarck, the train became snowbound in a blizzard too large for its two rotary snowplows. Kellogg, once a telegrapher, tapped into the wire and notified Fort Abraham Lincoln. Even though it took Tom Custer nearly a week, he arrived in a sleigh and rescued the Custers and their dogs, getting them to Bismarck a week before the train arrived.

Kellogg would file stories from Fort Abraham Lincoln and send back dispatches via military couriers as often as he could after the Dakota Column took the field. They provided the American public with news from the field nearly to the day of the Battle of the Little Bighorn.

## Dakota Column En Route

After being detained at Fort Abraham Lincoln by winter weather on the upper Great Plains, the Dakota Column at last was able to begin its trek to Montana on a cold Wednesday, May 17, 1876. Colonel Custer rode ahead of the advance guard—with one troop under his personal command and about forty Arikara and two half-Blackfeet scouts—to select the route. Army-supplied maps had only dotted lines showing likely routes of the major rivers and even more inaccurate locations for their tributaries. Like an Indian village traveling with their horses, the cavalry had to move along the routes that supplied water.

Elizabeth Custer estimated that 1,200 men—soldiers, around two hundred teamsters and herders, and more than forty scouts and translators—and 1,700 head of livestock (mules, horses, and beef cattle) made up the column that stretched two miles across the prairie. All twelve companies of the Seventh Cavalry were included, with two companies of the Seventh Infantry, one of the Sixth, and a platoon of Twentieth Infantry to man the three Gatling guns. Each of those cumbersome machine guns required four horses to pull its carriage. One hundred and fifty supply wagons carried forage for the horses, rations, ammunition, and other supplies. Custer's staghounds went along so he could enjoy hunting as he traveled.

The regimental band played the column off from "Fort A. Lincoln" with "Garryowen," an Irish jig probably suggested as a regimental song by Irish immigrant Captain Myles Keogh. The band's sixteen members would continue into the field on the steamboat *Far West*.

The men of the Seventh were divided into four battalions. Captain Frederick W. Benteen commanded the two battalions directly led by Captain Thomas B. Weir and Captain Thomas French, composed of Companies A, D, G, H, K, and M. Under Major Marcus A. Reno, Captain Keogh and Captain Yates commanded the other two, which included Companies B, C, E, F, I, and L.

*Captain Frederick W. Benteen. No date, photographer unidentified.*
COURTESY MONTANA HISTORICAL SOCIETY.

Each cavalry mount, along with its trooper, carried at least eighty pounds of gear and one hundred rounds of ammunition. With those loads, and the accompanying wagons and cattle, travel was slow. Reaching the Little Missouri River at the site of present-day Medora, North Dakota—ninety-four miles on today's Interstate 94— took thirteen days. Then the column turned south to explore up the river, where Terry expected to find the nontreaty Sioux and Northern Cheyennes.

Two days before the Dakota Column hit the trail, the Montana Column's Lieutenant James Bradley and his scouts had sighted the nontreaty village on the Tongue River, some 230 statute miles southwest of where General Terry reached the Little Missouri. By then, smaller bands of Sihasapa, Santee, and Brulé Sioux, and some Assiniboines, had joined the large village that was often on the move.

## Reno's Scout

After connecting with Colonel John Gibbon and the Montana Column at the mouth of the Powder River, Terry held his first meeting with Gibbon on the steamboat *Far West*. He assigned Major Marcus A. Reno, some scouts, and six cavalry companies to make a twelve-day scout up and down the tributaries of the Powder and Tongue rivers, ending where the Tongue met the Yellowstone. There the remainder of the Dakota Column would be waiting to act on Reno's discoveries. Terry emphasized that Reno was not to lead his men to Rosebud Creek, where the large village might see them. As soon as he saw any recent Indian trail, Reno was to head back to the Tongue River.

Sent with Reno was the excellent scout Mitch Boyer, who had been with the Montana Column until then and had been with Lieutenant Bradley when he first sighted the big village.

When Reno left on June 10, he thought the village would be on the Powder River, but Gibbon and Custer disagreed and worried that Reno's large command, with eleven mules per trooper, plus a Gatling gun on its carriage, would give away their presence. What the soldiers did not know was that the nontreaty Indians were well aware of all three army columns approaching them.

Eight days later, Major Reno and his men reached the Yellowstone River via Rosebud Creek, Reno having disobeyed Terry's orders. Possibly, as Terry wrote, Reno hoped to best his hated superior, Custer, by locating the nontreaty village and making "a successful attack...which would cover up his disobedience" (Stewart, p. 233).

Reno's most useful news was that he had seen no Indians at all in the valleys of the Powder, the Tongue, or the Rosebud, but had found a half-mile-wide trail made by a large number of horse-drawn travois, which led toward the Little Bighorn River. This discovery only confirmed what Lieutenant Bradley and the Crow scouts had been telling General Terry— but the general finally believed it when the word came from a higher officer.

At the time Reno turned his command around on June 16, the combined village of Sioux, Northern Cheyennes, and some Assiniboines may have included twelve thousand people in lodge circles that made a village extending for more than two miles (Stewart, p. 189). It was located near today's town of Busby, and moved westward as new land for horse grazing was needed.

In following the Indians' trail for thirty or so miles, Reno had

*Marcus A. Reno. No date, photograph by D. F. Barry.* COURTESY MONTANA HISTORICAL SOCIETY.

taken his men quite a bit closer to the village than he realized. Many of its warriors had gone away to fight Crook's Wyoming Column on Rosebud Creek on June 17, but plenty were left to take care of Reno's battalion. As Arikara scout Forked Horn told Reno upon viewing recent remains of a Sioux camp, if the troopers were seen "the sun will not move very far before we are all killed" (Libby, p. 71).

During Reno's scout, Major Orlando H. Moore moved all the Dakota Column's supplies, infantry troops, and band members up the Yellowstone River to the mouth of the Powder via the *Far West*. Custer scouted a trail over the badlands and led the wagon train there. Major Moore, some of the infantry, and the regimental band were to maintain a base camp where, among other duties, they would care for Custer's dogs. Cavalry members left their swords at the camp because the Indian response to a cavalry charge was to dissolve their line rather than to ride into it. Despite what dozens of illustrations depicted in the years following the battle, close fighting with sabers would not happen.

In response to Reno's scout, General Terry moved his command farther up the Yellowstone, near today's Forsyth at the mouth of Rosebud Creek. Colonel Gibbon's Montana Column bivouacked on the north side of the Yellowstone across from the Rosebud. Gibbon, expecting Terry's next move, now sent his troops back up toward Fort Pease across from the Bighorn's mouth.

## Attack Plan

Terry called a meeting of officers aboard the *Far West* on June 21 to outline his latest plan. Present were Custer of the Dakota Column, and Gibbon and Major James Brisbin of the Montana Column. All the officers expected General George Crook's Wyoming Column to be coming from the south, although there still had been no word from him. The minimal communications system consisted of a field commander (Crook in this case) sending couriers to a fort with a telegraph (Fort Fetterman in Wyoming, for Crook), which wired news to Sheridan's headquarters in Chicago. The reply was wired back, along with any orders, to the fort nearest the recipient. Terry was closest to Fort Ellis, but it was 220 miles west of his position. That fort's commander sent

*Captain Myles Keogh and his horse Comanche. Date unknown.*
COURTESY DENVER PUBLIC LIBRARY, WESTERN HISTORY COLLECTION, DAVID FRANCES PHOTO, B-336.

couriers to deliver the message into the field. Therefore, the officers on the *Far West* had no idea that Crook had been defeated only four days previously, and that he and his men now were hunting and fishing while they awaited reinforcements and food supplies.

Terry's plan was for the Montana Column to march to the mouth of the Bighorn River, where the *Far West* would ferry the men across. Turning south up the Bighorn, they would almost immediately come to Tullock Creek and start upstream along its rugged banks. Tullock flows north and slightly west out of the Wolf Mountains, east of the Little Bighorn, and was where Terry then thought the big village stood.

Grant Marsh was to take the *Far West*, with Captain Stephen Baker's Sixth Infantry company aboard, up the Yellowstone and, after ferrying the Montana Column across the Yellowstone, continue up the Bighorn. The latter was something no steamboat had done before, and even Captain Marsh was not sure he could succeed. But his orders were to proceed to the mouth of the Little Bighorn at today's Hardin, then hold the boat there as a supply depot and hospital.

Meanwhile, Custer was to take the entire Seventh Cavalry up Rosebud Creek (east of the Bighorn River), moving slowly and constantly scouting his left flank for Indians arriving from the east or south. When he found the large Indian trail that Reno had reported, he was to cross it and continue a bit farther south before heading west and then north toward the upper Little Bighorn. Custer's extra travel time was to compensate for the cavalry's speed compared to that of Gibbon's infantry (Stewart, p. 241).

The two commands did not intend to cross this badlands area and meet to make a joint attack. Terry's and Gibbon's men coming from the north would be positioned to stop Indians fleeing from Custer's men. The officers on the *Far West* fully expected that Crook was coming from the south, and even worried that he might engage the Indians while they still were moving into position. Terry's and Gibbon's important duty was to prevent the Indians from moving north to the Yellowstone—or beyond it to the Missouri River. Part of Custer's job was to block them from fleeing south to sanctuary in the Big Horn Mountains or back to the Great Sioux Reservation (the latter, of course, being the entire campaign's publicly stated goal). Even though the Crow and Arikara scouts insisted that the Sioux and North Cheyennes could field as many as five thousand warriors, the officers projected only five hundred to one thousand or fifteen hundred—the high figure being Custer's estimate.

After the meeting, reporter Kellogg sent a dispatch out via courier (not realizing it would be his last), expecting that it would appear in newspapers on June 22. He wrote that "today" troops were moving on the village. Gibbon's aide Lieutenant James H. Bradley wrote in his journal that "it is understood that if Custer arrives first he is at liberty to attack at once if he deems prudent." Knowing Custer's reputation, Bradley expected that Custer would "undoubtedly exert himself to the utmost to get there first and win all the laurels for himself and his regiment" (Stewart, p. 246). The Second Cavalry's Lieutenant Edward J. McClernand later wrote of "Custer's aggressive temperament" and that his "custom had always been to throw himself upon his foe, like a hound on a rabbit..." (McClernand, p. 94).

Terry assigned to Custer the half-Sioux scout Mitch Boyer and Gibbon's best Crow scouts, because they knew this country so much better than did the Arikaras. The Crows, who volunteered for the duty, were Half Yellow Face, White Swan, White-Man-Runs-Him, Hairy Moccasin, Goes Ahead, and Curley. Custer also took the Arikara scouts, whom he had admired and trusted for years, including one whom he called "my favorite scout, Bloody Knife," as he had recently written in his *The Galaxy* article. Bloody Knife's father was Sioux and his mother Arikara, and he had spent his early boyhood living with the Sioux before his mother moved back to her people, apparently later marrying a Northern Cheyenne.

*Curley. No date, photograph by O. S. Goff.*
COURTESY MONTANA HISTORICAL SOCIETY.

Terry added civilian scout "Lonesome" Charley Reynolds and inter-preter Isaiah Dorman. Reynolds had been with Custer in the Black Hills two years before and was the courier who had carried out Custer's dis-patch about gold finds there. Dorman, an escaped slave who had mar-ried a Santee Sioux woman, had been a mail carrier, scout, and post interpreter at Fort Rice, near Bismarck. Custer took another interpreter, former trader to the Arikaras Frederic F. Gerard, hired at Fort Abraham Lincoln. Terry sent George Herendeen as a courier (with bonus pay) whose orders were to leave Custer after the Tullock Creek scout, go down that creek to the Yellowstone, and tell Terry what Custer had found. If the trustworthy Herendeen—an "unusually reliable man" in Lieutenant McClernand's opinion (McClernand, p. 37)—could not go, Custer was to send a different courier.

Behind the scouts, Custer would lead about 585 enlisted men under thirty-one officers. Each trooper carried fifteen days' rations for himself and twelve pounds of oats for his horse, plus one hundred rounds of carbine ammunition and twenty-four rounds for his pistol. Custer assigned 1st Lieutenant Edward G. Mathey to command the pack train that contained 175 mules (which were accustomed to pulling wagons, not carrying packs), seventy troopers, and seven civilian packers including Boston Custer and Autie Reed. The lucky Mark Kellogg was the sole reporter taken along. The command started out with the Gatling guns, but Custer soon sent them back because their wagons were too cumbersome and slow over the rough, shrub-covered ground.

## Marching by Day and Night

The Seventh Cavalry moved out at noon on June 22 and headed up Rosebud Creek, again played off by the regimental band. By the end of the next day, Custer found the trail Reno had reported and the Rosebud village site Bradley had seen. He noticed many small wickiups along the way, which he and his men thought were dog houses. They might have been more vigilant if they had believed the Indian scouts, who informed them that young, single warriors used this type of shelter.

Terry, Gibbon, and Brisbin rode aboard the *Far West*, which traveled from midday until dark, then left again early in the morning of June 23 and reached Fort Pease at 6 A.M. the next day. Gibbon's infantry had a head start and reached Fort Pease first, with his cavalry troops only two miles behind. On June 24, the *Far West* ferried twelve Crow scouts across the Yellowstone before noon (Lieutenant Bradley crossed soon after and caught up with them), then spent most of the afternoon ferrying the Montana Column across. The troopers headed up the Bighorn River, leaving their commander Colonel Gibbon, who just had become ill, on board where he stayed for two more days. General Terry replaced Gibbon and led the Montana Column.

Grant Marsh forced the *Far West* to drag itself up the Bighorn—shallow but swift here on its lower end—from after noon until 8:30 P.M. on June 25. He tied ropes from the two capstans to trees ahead on each bank, then used the steamboat's power to reel the ropes in, pulling the shallow-draft boat along. On June 26, Marsh pulled out at 3:30 A.M. Six hours later, Gibbon left the *Far West* and rode to catch up with Terry. The *Far West* progressed slowly until nine o'clock that night, when it was still eight hours away from the Little Bighorn. On June 27, when Marsh announced they had reached their goal, Captain Stephen Baker disagreed and ordered the boat to continue upstream. Marsh obeyed and continued upstream all day before getting permission to turn back. The boat finally tied up at the Little Bighorn on June 28.

Early in the morning of June 24, Custer and the Seventh Cavalry heard from their Crow scouts that fresh Sioux tracks had appeared near camp. Continuing to move up Rosebud Creek on a hot day in the cloud of dust that their horses raised, they passed the site where the big village's Sioux residents had held their Sun Dance on about June 9 through 14. Later, while crossing Tullock Creek, Colonel Custer refused to let Herendeen go report their sighting to General Terry, stating that there was no news to take now but he would let Herendeen earn his promised bonus as soon as there was. Custer also ignored Terry's order to scout up Tullock Creek.

Tactically, that decision was not as dangerous as Custer's next one. He halted the command at 8:00 P.M. near today's Busby, on Rosebud Creek and east of the steep but low hills called the Wolf Mountains. He and his men were much farther along than Terry had wanted them to be by this time. Both the troopers and their mounts were tired after traveling thirty miles in the day's heat. Custer sent Goes Ahead, Hairy Moccasin, and White-Man-Runs-Him ahead to scout. They returned and said they had not seen the big village. Custer ordered a night march to begin at 11:00 P.M.—even though his orders were to take his time approaching the village so that Terry and Gibbon could get into position from the north. And even though both man and beast needed sleep.

While the Seventh took its brief rest, Custer sent his chief of scouts, 2nd Lieutenant Charles Varnum, with Mitch Boyer, Charley Reynolds, and about ten other scouts to a favorite Crow vantage point atop the Wolf Mountains. Nicknamed "the Crow's Nest" by whites, the spot gave a distant view of the Little Bighorn River valley. It took the men until 2:30 A.M. on June 25 to reach the Crow's Nest, where they waited and watched as pre-dawn light strengthened in the east. At last, Varnum could see smoke hovering over a village he thought was twenty miles away (Boyer thought the distance fifteen miles). Even with his field glasses, he could not make out more than that, but the scouts were talking in amazement about the largest pony herd they had ever seen and all the lodges standing on the flat river bottom. At about 5:00 A.M., Varnum sent Arikara scouts Red Star and Bull to inform Custer. On their way, they saw a few Sioux scouts both in front of and behind Custer's men. The Sioux hurried for the village, riding their horses in circles to warn that enemies were near.

At the beginning of their night march, the men of the Seventh could see nothing in the moonless dark and kept in line by following the scent of dust kicked up by the horses ahead. Getting the pack animals across Muddy Creek delayed their start until after midnight, so Custer then had each company lead its own mules. They moved west into the Wolf Mountains, upstream along Davis Creek. After crossing the crest, their path would be downstream on today's Reno Creek. But the scouts said they would not be able to cross the top before daybreak, and then they would be silhouetted on the horizon.

Custer halted the column at about 2:00 A.M., and the men and horses hid in one of the Wolf Mountains' many deep ravines. He said they would wait out the day and finish crossing that night, even though the water here was so alkaline that the thirsty horses refused to drink. Such a wait would have put his column closer to the schedule Terry had outlined—reaching the village on June 26—and the general and his troops would have been nearby.

But then Red Star arrived with the news of the vast village and the Sioux scouts watching Custer's command. Bloody Knife, who was standing beside Custer along with Frederic Gerard and Half Yellow Face, told the colonel that "there were more hostiles ahead than there were bullets in the belts of the soldiers" (Stewart, p. 274). He added that it could take three days to fight all these warriors, but Custer answered that a day would be enough. Having been discovered meant the cavalry had to attack that day, so he gave orders to move out, and the Seventh was on its way before 9:00 A.M. on June 25. Privately, Custer told his officers that he doubted there even was a village on the Little

Bighorn, but they had to deal with whoever was tracking them.

Custer sent his scouts ahead to try to stampede the nontreaty Indians' horse herd. To guard their own animals, Custer divided his company for the first time and assigned Captain Thomas M. McDougall and Company B to go back and protect the supply train. The train was to move forward at the mules' own pace.

Custer joined Varnum at the Crow's Nest, but he, too, could not make out the village the scouts were describing. The two officers actually thought the village was starting to break up when they saw about sixty lodges moving near Reno Creek, but these people really were just arriving.

Seeing the Crow scouts painting themselves for battle, Custer asked through Boyer, "Why are you doing all this?" Half Yellow Face stood up to show respect and said, "Because you and I are going home today, by a trail that is strange to all of us." Painting his face, donning his best clothing, and arranging his hair were not to aid an Indian warrior's fighting but were done in case he was killed. The Cheyenne warrior Wooden Leg, sixteen when he fought Custer's troops, explained that a man wanted "to look his best when he goes to meet the Great Spirit" (Viola, p. 41).

Other preparations were made for protection. Young Hawk, a teenaged Arikara scout for Custer, later recalled that the Arikaras' own leader, Stabbed, had brought "clay...from our home country," around Bismarck. Stabbed now moistened and prayed over the clay.

*Then he called up the young men and had us hold up our shirts in front so that he could rub the good medicine on our bodies.... I unbraided my hair, brought it forward on my head, and tied it with...eagle feathers. I expected to be killed and scalped by the Sioux, and I wanted to be ready to die. (Viola, p. 32)*

Charley Reynolds parceled out his belongings in farewell to his comrades. Only the cavalry troops were in a joking mood as the march began, excited about "action" even in their tired state.

Although the troopers would not have perceived it this way, they too prepared by changing their appearances. Officers, especially, removed their coats, shirts, and hats, ridding themselves of badges of rank because they knew that Indians could read brass insignia and chevron or rocker stripes. Colonel Custer, called Long Hair by the Sioux, wore an enlisted man's company cap covering his short-cut, receding blond hair and a blue flannel shirt above buckskin pants (Stewart, p. 274). Captain Tom Custer and 1st Lieutenant James Porter were among those wearing buckskin shirts; Tom Custer added a white hat (Stewart, pp. 415, 464).

The companies' positions in the line—which would determine each trooper's fate in battle—were assigned as each commander announced his men ready to go. Captain Benteen and Company H were first. At about noon on a hot, bright, dry June 25, the Seventh crossed the top of the Wolf Mountains and began down into the village on the Little Bighorn. Lieutenant Varnum and his scouts left the Crow's Nest to fall in.

At that same time, the Montana Column's Lieutenant James Bradley and his scouts had left Terry's command and started up Tullock Creek, to the northeast. But, with no news from Custer, Terry changed his plan and decided to continue upstream on the Bighorn. He sent for Bradley and the scouts to rejoin the command.

## Attack and Retreat: Reno

The Sioux and Northern Cheyenne village sat along a stretch of the Little Bighorn that flowed generally from southeast to northwest, making many loops along the way. To the Sioux, Cheyennes, and Crows, the waterway was the "Greasy Grass." The young Oglala Sioux (and future holy man) Black Elk and Chief Red Horse, a Minneconjou Sioux, remembered the sequence of lodge circles differently, but both placed the Hunkpapa circle farthest south (closest to Reno Creek), with the Oglalas, Minneconjous, and the Cheyennes in sequence north, or downstream.

In the village's lodges and one-man wickiups were around four thousand warriors by historian Edgar I. Stewart's estimate, or perhaps fewer than two thousand according to Blackfeet novelist James Welch's more recent book, *Killing Custer*. At any rate, Custer rode toward the village with fewer than five hundred troopers.

The early June snow had added to the Little Bighorn's flow, which ran fast and at places deep enough to swim a horse. Today's visitors see much shallower water, because some from upstream is diverted for irrigation. On that day of June 25, horses could ford the Little Bighorn only at three places by the village: the mouth of Reno Creek to the south, the bottom of Medicine Tail Coulee opposite the village's middle, and about a mile farther north across from the Cheyenne lodge circle.

Reaching the headwaters of Reno Creek on the west side of the Wolf Mountains, about fifteen miles away from the village Custer still had not seen, he divided his command for the second time. He ordered Captain Benteen to take Company H under himself, D under Captain Thomas B. Weir, and K under Lieutenant 1st Edward S. Godfrey and sweep left. They were to look for the mysterious village, keep Indians from fleeing, watch for Crook's expected column, and notify Custer about what they saw. These officers and their men rode away at a quarter past twelve and were out of sight in a quarter of an hour.

Benteen would ride about five miles before deciding his mission was futile and angle back toward the Little Bighorn. Just as he turned, shortly before 3:00 P.M., Boston Custer rode by and waved; he had gone ahead of the pack train to join his brother.

Continuing down Reno Creek after Benteen had left, the rest of the Dakota Column soon saw around fifty Indians, women and children with a rear guard of warriors, riding away (toward the big village) from what has become known as the "Lone Tipi." They were part of the band Varnum had spied from the Crow's Nest, just coming to join the village, and had camped here overnight. The tipi was a Sioux burial lodge that had been built when the big village sat here, possibly for a warrior mortally wounded in the Battle of Rosebud Creek the week before. As they passed, the soldiers set it afire.

Custer then divided his command for the third time. His adjutant, Lieutenant William W. Cooke, delivered Custer's order that Major Reno peel off Companies A, G, and M—120 to 140 men—and cross the Little Bighorn, then attack this small group of Indians. Reno later said that Custer's message included the promise to support him. All the scouts except Boyer, four Crows, and one or two Arikaras went with Reno.

Now Custer directly commanded only about 215 men, in five of the Seventh Cavalry's twelve companies: C, E, F, I, and L. Company E later was called by both Indians and whites the "gray horse troop," because most of its troopers had been given the regimental band's matched animals to ride that day.

Reno and his men easily crossed the Little Bighorn at the ford by the mouth of Reno Creek, which made them believe that all the Little Bighorn was shallower than it was. As soon as they were gone, chief of scouts Varnum arrived to tell Custer he had seen the village, and it was big. Instead of following Reno, Custer led his men—their horses trotting at normal speed—to the right and behind the bluffs, parallel to the Little Bighorn. Chief Gall, a Hunkpapa war chief, said he saw Custer's troops across the river and up above, and thought they were making a "parade," or ceremonial approach (Stewart, p. 347). He said that approach made him believe their intentions were peaceful.

Reno's command trotted along the west side of the Little Bighorn and, in three miles, could see the Hunkpapa lodges of the village's southern end. He immediately sent his striker (personal servant), Private Archibald McIlhargy, to Custer to report that many more Indians were here than any of the officers had believed. Reno continued moving along the sandy river bottom, convinced Custer would soon follow.

Even though Indians in the village knew soldiers were near, they did not expect an attack. Young men had been racing horses on the flat beside the Little Bighorn. Chief Red Horse, one of the council leaders, was a mile south with four women, harvesting wild turnips, when one of the women alerted him to Reno's approaching dust cloud.

At about 3:00 P.M., the battle began as Reno charged the nearest tipis and his men shot into the Hunkpapa lodges, setting some of them on fire. Chief Gall's two wives and his three children were killed instantly.

*Chief Red Horse rushed to the council lodge in the village's center, where the leaders tried to hold council, but Reno was coming too fast. "The soldiers charged so quickly we could not talk," he said. "We came out of the council lodge and called in all directions: 'Young men—mount horses and take guns; go fight the soldiers.*

*Women and children—mount horses and go, get out of the way.'"*
*(Viola, p. 33)*

Standing by his lodge, Sitting Bull shouted, "Warriors, we have everything to fight for, and if we are defeated we shall have nothing to live for, therefore let us fight like brave men" (Stewart, p. 349).

*Iron Hawk, a teenaged Hunkpapa, had slept late, probably having enjoyed the social dance the night before, and was just eating breakfast outside his lodge when he heard a camp-crier's warning. He got dressed for war "as fast as I could, but I could hear bullets whizzing outside. I was so shaky that it took me a long time to braid an eagle feather into my hair. I also had to hold my pony's rope all the time, and he kept jerking me and trying to get away."*
*(Viola, p. 37)*

Wooden Leg's father kept shouting for him to hurry up while the teen rushed into new breeches, a "good cloth shirt" and beaded moccasins, and painted his face and tied back his hair.

The Indian warriors grabbed their mixture of new guns, old guns, clubs, and bows and arrows. Oglala Chief Low Dog, awakened in his lodge by a crier, said, "I heard the alarm, but I did not believe it.... I did not think it possible that any white man would attack us, so strong as we were" (Viola, p. 35).

He went outside and watched the Hunkpapas hold their ground "to give the women and children time to get out of the way." He said, "By this time our herders were driving in our horses, and our men were catching them and hurrying to go and help those that were fighting." When the fighters saw that the women and children were safe, they fell back (Viola, p. 71).

Reno thought they were setting a trap and halted his troops, ordering them to dismount and fight on foot—one hundred or fewer yards from the village's edge. He sent a second man to find Custer, cook Private John Mitchell, with the same message that McIlhargy had carried. By then Custer's battalion was close to being across from the village's center, where the bluffs hiding them curved farther away from the river. Some Indians and white men present thought that if Reno had continued his charge all the way through the village, it would have demoralized the Sioux. But some of Reno's own soldiers believed the Sioux and Cheyennes would have killed the entire command.

Chiefs Gall and One Bull led the Hunkpapas in fighting Reno's troops. They soon had reinforcements as warriors raced through the village. The Sioux and Northern Cheyennes blew eagle-bone whistles, bullets whizzed, dust and gunsmoke filled the hot air. Warriors shouted the war rallying call, "It is a good day to die! Strong hearts, brave hearts, to the front!" and the Cheyennes yelled taunts. Even if they had understood the language, the Dakota Column would not have understood why the Cheyennes were yelling, as Wooden Leg said: "We whipped you on the Rosebud. You should have brought more Crows or Shoshones with you to do your fighting" (Viola, p. 43).

Up behind the bluffs across the Little Bighorn, Custer had sent Sergeant Daniel Kanipe back to the pack train, ordering it to speed up with the ammunition supply. He moved to the bluff tops to look down, but even when he finally glimpsed the village, intervening bluffs still hid its full extent. Custer also could see Reno's troops riding toward the village (Stewart, p. 337).

When Reno had his men dismount and form a skirmish line, he had to assign thirty men to hold the horses, each one forced to control four excited animals. Now he had only around one hundred fighting men against his estimate of five hundred to six hundred Indian warriors in this part of the village. The horse-holders moved into a grove of trees and brush along the riverbank, and after fifteen to twenty minutes of constant shooting Reno ordered the rest of his men into the trees. In another quarter of an hour, Sioux warriors began moving into the trees and underbrush, trying to flank the troops. When Sergeant John M. Ryan notified his superior, Thomas French, the captain told him not to worry—it was Custer's men arriving.

Nearly surrounded, with no sign yet of Custer, Reno ordered the men to retreat by fording the Little Bighorn, where two- to three-hundred-foot bluffs beckoned. As Companies A and M started to move, they stopped firing, which let the hidden Sioux come thirty feet closer through the heavy brush. Bloody Knife was reporting to Reno when a Sioux bullet hit him between the eyes. His face splattered with the blood and brains of Custer's favorite scout, Reno reacted instantly. He spurred his horse to the river, and most of his men immediately joined in a disorganized, unprotected rout.

Here the Little Bighorn was nowhere near as shallow as at the Reno Creek ford. Soldiers pushed their horses down a steep five-foot cutbank, only to discover that the creek's water came up to their saddles. On the far side, the mounts had to make their way up an eight-foot cutbank. The frightened horses were hard to control and could not cross quickly.

For about fifteen minutes, they and their riders made relatively slow-moving targets for Indian shooters. Troopers fell from their saddles and fought hand to hand. Warriors swam into the water, pulled other troopers from their saddles, and clubbed them to death.

Left behind at the village were Reno's dead and wounded, some scouts including would-be messenger George Herendeen, 1st Lieutenant Charles C. DeRudio and sixteen enlisted men who had not heard the order to retreat. "Lonesome" Charley Reynolds left the trees to catch up while providing covering fire, but he and his horse were killed immediately. Isaiah Dorman made it closer to the water before the Sioux surrounded him. Chief Runs-the-Enemy said that Dorman kept firing his gun even after he and his horse had suffered multiple wounds (Stewart, p. 370).

Wooden Leg and other warriors saw that "The soldier horses moved slowly, as if they were very tired. Ours were lively. We gained rapidly on them" (Viola, p. 43). The Cheyennes were amazed at the cavalry's leaving the trees' safety to come back out into the open. The Cheyennes would have been content to contain the soldiers and keep them out of the battle, although the Sioux were ready to invade the trees.

Warriors all around fired at Reno's disorganized, retreating cavalry as they struggled across the river, up the bank, and on up through a ravine to the hilltop more than two hundred feet above the Little Bighorn. By the time Reno's men took this barely defensible point, around 4:00 P.M., fewer than one hundred of them survived. As the soldiers fired outward from the top, some Indians scaled higher bluffs to snipe at them.

Numerous ravines on the hill offered cover for warriors who wanted to climb it, but for now none did. Most of them headed down the Little Bighorn to join those fighting against Custer's command. Now called Reno Hill, Reno's defense site is near the town of Garryowen.

## Attack and Retreat: Custer

Custer reached the top of Medicine Tail Coulee while Reno's men still were engaged in the valley. This wide ravine angles northwest, down to reach the ford where the center of the village was located. Here Custer had Mitch Boyer release the Crow scouts, their mission accomplished. White-Man-Runs-Him, Goes Ahead, and Hairy Moccasin rode off and eventually joined the other battalion on Reno Hill, but Curley remained. Heading down the coulee, Custer ordered Private Giovanni Martini, an immigrant trumpeter whose name on the rolls had been Americanized to John Martin, to find Benteen and call him—and all his ammunition packs—in from the searching sweep. Obviously upset, adjutant Cooke scribbled out the message for Martini: "Benteen. Come on. Big Village. Be Quick. Bring packs. W.W. Cooke. P.S. Bring pacs" (Stewart, p. 340).

Coming down the rough coulee toward the river, Custer and his men met a great number of Sioux warriors led by Chief Gall, who had crossed the Little Bighorn to stop their progress and protect the village. How close Custer's battalion got to the water is uncertain. None of Custer's battalion survived; it was out of sight from Reno's and Benteen's commands, and Indian accounts disagree. Cheyenne war chief Brave Wolf said that the fighting there—not quite at the Little Bighorn's edge and definitely across from the village—lasted a long time (Stewart, p. 441). Even though the broken hillside was not good for cavalry fighting, the soldiers stayed on their horses, firing into the larger force of Indians.

Army artifacts found at the Medicine Tail Coulee ford have convinced some scholars that part of Custer's command reached the Little Bighorn. But other scholars argue that those very items could have been dropped near the ford after being taken from dead soldiers anywhere on the battlefield (Scott, *Perspectives*, pp. 17,19).

The soldiers were being driven uphill to their right, up Deep Coulee, which runs southwest-northeast. Brave Wolf said there were "so many people around them that they could not help being killed. They still held their line of battle, and kept fighting and falling from their horses—fighting and falling…" (Grinnell, p. 340).

Indian bullets and arrows also found many cavalry horses, leaving their riders on foot. Brave Wolf thought that no horses reached the top alive, but some were found lying next to troopers' bodies, their carcasses having been used as barricades. Sitting Bull later said, "When they rode up, their horses were tired and they were tired," just as Wooden Leg had said. But, Sitting Bull added, "When they got off from their horses, they could not stand firmly on their feet. They swayed to and fro—so my young men have told me…" (Viola, p. 60).

During Custer's retreat up the coulee, Curley finally accepted Boyer's dismissal and made his way east, slipping through ravines on foot and then riding a captured Sioux horse. From a hilltop, he used his army field glasses to watch Custer's battle for a while, then left to return to Terry's command with the news. For days his fellow Crows would think him killed.

Those still alive in Custer's battalion who reached the top of the bluffs ran into warriors that Crazy Horse had led in a sweep (up the confusingly named Deep Ravine, which runs northwest-southeast) from the northern end of the village. Warriors were coming from all sides. The troopers clustered by company and took the defensive positions in which most of them died. Soldiers who heard the shooting from down in the grove of trees and atop Reno Hill and the Indians who were fighting estimated the length of this "last stand" at about fifteen to forty-five minutes.

Chief Red Horse recalled that

*When we attacked [Custer's] party, we swarmed down on them and drove them in confusion. Some soldiers became panic-stricken, throwing down their guns and raising up their hands, saying, "Sioux, pity us; take us prisoners." The Sioux did not take a single soldier prisoner, but killed all of them. None were left alive even for a few minutes. (Viola, p. 50)*

Chief Gall led warriors who wiped out Company L, under Margaret Custer's husband, Lieutenant James Calhoun, and which was closest to Deep Coulee. They moved on to Captain Myles Keogh's Company I, which was still coming up a ravine to the ridge. Gall's warriors moved north, and Indians led by Chief Low Dog and Chief Crow King came uphill from the west. They found Company C, under Captain Thomas Custer and Company E, temporarily led by 1st Lieutenant Algernon E. Smith of Company A (which was with Reno), hidden in a ravine. Then they killed Captain George W. Yates and his men in Company F right on the ridge.

Farthest from Deep Coulee and north of Deep Ravine were Colonel George Armstrong Custer and about fifty men, including troopers who had run that way as their own companies were attacked. The bodies around Custer included his youngest brother, Boston—who, ignoring orders, had joined George—namesake nephew Autie Reed, reporter Kellogg, adjutant Cooke, and Sergeant Robert Hughes, detached from Company K in Benteen's relatively safe command to carry Custer's battle flag that day. Also found there were Reno's two messengers, privates McIlhargy and Mitchell.

Throughout the uphill battle, Brave Wolf said, "It was hard fighting; very hard all the time. I have been in many hard fights, but I never saw such brave men" (Grinnell, p. 340).

## Siege

After greeting Boston Custer, Benteen's command had come to the wide trail the village had made as it progressed down the Little Bighorn and started following it to reach the other battalions. When Benteen passed the Lone Tipi, it was still burning. Sergeant Kanipe, carrying Colonel Custer's message to the pack train, shouted "We've got them, boys!"—leaving the impression that Custer had attacked the village.

At about 3:00 P.M. by Benteen's estimate, and about a mile from where Reno's survivors were scrambling up the bluff, trumpeter messenger Martini galloped up. Benteen pointed out that his horse was bleeding badly from a bullet wound, which the private had not noticed. Although Martini delivered the note, he did not think to tell Benteen of the Indians he had seen rushing at Custer as he rode away or that when he passed Reno's command, he had seen them engaged in serious fighting. In the few moments before Martini rode on to the pack train, 2nd Lieutenant Winfield S. Edgerly heard him telling troopers that Reno had charged the village and "was killing everybody—men, women, and children" (Stewart, p. 384).

Benteen's men galloped toward the village with pistols drawn and saw most Indians racing downstream ahead of them—but he did not know they were moving from Reno toward Custer. Benteen rode on alone to the central ford, passing Reno's ill-fated crossing place. From there he now could see "that two fights seemed to be going on at the same time, one in the valley and the other on the bluffs" (Stewart, p. 388). The dozen or so dismounted troopers who had finally formed a skirmish line down by the river were protecting others still climbing Reno Hill. Benteen returned to his three companies and led them across the Little Bighorn and up the bluff. They reached Reno even before all of Reno's command had crossed the river.

Benteen's immediate assessment was that Reno's battalion was "shaken." He saw its commander shooting a pistol, effective only at close range, and Lieutenant Varnum crying while firing his carbine in every direction. Not everyone was out of control, though: Captain Weir's Company D had returned Indian sharpshooters' bullets and driven them away from a higher bluff.

Reno and Benteen agreed that the Indians' run to the north probably was an attempt to draw them into an ambush, and so they stayed put on the hilltop. In a half hour or so, there were no Indians in sight, so Reno took a burial detail down to the flat to inter the soldiers who had fallen crossing the Little Bighorn. In this group was Captain Weir, who argued angrily with his superior that they should instead be riding to Custer's aid.

One of the battle's great questions is whether Reno and Benteen believed their colonel could use help but stayed away because of personal animosity. Benteen later testified that he could hear no gunfire to the north. Although the Bozeman newspaper soon wrote that scout Muggins Taylor mentioned Reno's having "heard the first and last volleys of the firing" against Custer, there is no proof that either Reno or Taylor made the statement. If Custer's junior officers did indeed hear the fighting on "Last Stand Hill," duty required them to try to head in that direction.

Leaving without permission, Weir and his orderly went back up the bluff and headed north to try to locate Custer. Lieutenant Edgerly and Company C, assuming Weir's movement was sanctioned, followed for about a mile and a half atop the bluffs. They stopped at what is now called Weir Point, looking north to a hill "obscured by a great cloud of dust and smoke..." and seeing "Indians riding around and shooting at objects on the ground." Lieutenant Varnum saw "some white objects that [he] thought were rocks, but found afterward they were naked bodies of men" (Carroll, p. 92). Indians coming up a nearby ravine drove Weir and Edgerly back to Reno's location.

Not long after Benteen's command had reached Reno Hill, Captain McDougall arrived with Company B and the supply train. Now there were blankets and some medical supplies for the wounded, a few tools, and the rest of the Seventh Cavalry's ammunition. About 350 soldiers, civilians, and scouts, including Half Yellow Face and White Swan with half of one hand shot off, were gathered on the hilltop.

Even though Reno was still nominally in command of what remained of his assigned Companies A, G, and M, he seemed incapable of making up his mind about what to do. Benteen, who was the Seventh's senior captain anyway, in effect took charge of all seven companies and is credited for saving the men who survived the hilltop siege. Only a few minutes after Weir began his scout against Reno's wishes, Benteen took three companies and started out in Weir's tracks, intending to yell and wave from the ridge to let Custer know their position. Benteen told the Reno Court of Inquiry later that he planted a guidon on Weir Point in the hope that Custer would see it (Stewart, p. 403). Reno and the rest of his command followed Benteen.

Having finished with Custer's command, the Sioux and Northern Cheyennes came back for the rest of the troops. Benteen wanted to seek a better defensive position, but Reno argued for the familiar hilltop. The soldiers just made it back to Reno Hill before being surrounded—the men of Company K, at the rear, tumbling in and landing wherever they could find spots. It was now around 7:00 P.M. and about three hours of light remained on this northern midsummer day.

The men's hope now was to last until Custer returned—or Terry's or Crook's command arrived. While some of the men believed Custer's command must be surrounded, many—including officers—thought he had attacked the village, been turned away, and simply left to join Terry.

## Spoils of the Battlefield

While the warriors pushed the Reno-Benteen command back, the village's other members followed custom and began to strip and mutilate the bodies of Custer's men. Black Elk was with women and other young people who "went to the top of the hill. Gray horses were lying dead there, and some of them were on top of dead soldiers, and dead soldiers were on top of them. After a while I got tired looking around. I could smell nothing but blood, and I got sick of it" (Viola, p. 63).

But as for the big victory, Black Elk "was not sorry at all." He said, "I was a happy boy. Those white soldiers had come to kill our mothers and fathers and us, and it was our country" (Viola, p. 63).

Sitting Bull again preached his rejection of white culture:

*I warned my people not to touch the spoils of the battlefield, not to take the guns and horses from the dead soldiers. Many did not heed, and it will prove a curse to this nation. Indians who set their hearts upon the goods of the white man will be at his mercy and will starve at his hands (Viola, p. 66).*

The Sioux and Cheyenne practice of taking and using vanquished warriors' goods was nearly fatal to Lieutenant DeRudio the following dawn. He and the men still hiding in the trees down beside the Little Bighorn heard horses approaching and saw that they were the unusual gray of Company E's mounts. One rider had on a buckskin shirt and a white hat, so DeRudio thought it was Captain Tom Custer. DeRudio stepped out in the clear and called to him. Nothing. Then DeRudio yelled, "Here I am, don't you see me?" and the Indian rider looked up and shot at him (Stewart, p. 415). Unknown to DeRudio, Tom Custer's scalped, mutilated corpse then lay on Last Stand Hill.

For the Sioux and Northern Cheyennes in battle, counting coup—touching an enemy—was even more honorable than killing him. Mutilating the dead afterwards, which was done to Indians as well as whites, was part of victory, a way of giving a lesson to their dead enemies that also affected how they would appear and act in the afterlife. Two young Northern Cheyenne women found an Indian corpse whose clothing mixed items of the Arikaras (their traditional enemies) and the white soldiers. He obviously had been an Indian scout for the cavalry. They decapitated him and carried the head back to camp on a pole, showing it around. When they approached their mother, she saw the head of her own brother, the girls' disowned half-uncle, Bloody Knife.

Two of the few Southern Cheyenne women in the village came upon the corpse of a soldier they had seen years before in the south—Long Hair, Colonel George A. Custer. Chief Low Dog said, "They pushed the point of a bone sewing awl through his ear. They did this to improve his hearing in the spirit world. He must not have listened very well in this life, or he would have heard what our chiefs said about broken promises" (Viola, p. 71). The army suppressed information about this and other mutilations until after the death of Elizabeth Custer, the widow, in 1933.

That night, while a handful of warriors surrounded Reno Hill to keep the soldiers from escaping, most of the village either celebrated victory or mourned for their dead. Large fires burned and drums beat as dancers recounted the day's battle. Elsewhere keening came from relatives of slain warriors. A little rain fell over the village and the nearby hilltop.

How many Indians died is unknown because their custom was to immediately remove bodies from the battlefield. Five years later, Chief Low Dog told reporters that thirty-eight Indians were killed and "a great many—I can't tell the number" (Utley) were wounded, proportionately more than usual. Many of the wounded died later as the village moved away. Estimates of the Indian dead, depending upon the source, reach as high as three hundred.

Chief Gall, interviewed at the tenth anniversary commemoration of the battle, was asked how many Indians had died. "Forty-three in all.... They [the wounded] died every day. Nearly as many died each day as were killed in the fight. We buried them in trees and on scaffolds…" (Utley).

## The Second Day

Atop Reno Hill, the troopers dug in after darkness fell and the firing stopped. Some used butcher knives and the pack train's shovels and axes to dig trenches in the sandy soil, while others had to use their lightweight tin mess kits and cups or their hands. They dragged dead mules and horses to the summit's perimeter and placed them legs outward, then tied the carcasses together with scavenged bits of rope. Cavalry saddles, pack saddles, bags of bacon, and crates added to this makeshift breastwork. After taking the hilltop, the civilian packers had been told to protect the livestock in the natural indentation in the hilltop's center. That freed the horse-holders for defense on both days of the siege.

What sleep the besieged men got that night came only from their sheer exhaustion. As Lieutenant Varnum recalled,

> I was thoroughly exhausted. I had ridden about seventy miles on the 24th and had only about an hour's sleep at the Crow Nest that night. About 10 o'clock [on June 25] I lay down on the edge of the bluffs and must have gone to sleep at once. I was awakened by being carried somewhere, and found myself in the arms of old "Tony" [Anton] Siebelder of Troop A. It seems I had gone to sleep at an exposed point and when daylight broke [on June 26], old "Tony" saw my danger & was carrying me to a safer place…. (Carroll, p. 93)

In the center atop Reno Hill was Dr. Henry Porter's field hospital, which began to receive more wounded as soon as daylight arrived and sniping began again. Indians shot guns down from higher bluffs and sent arrows arcing in from other hiding places. Sometimes Reno's men returned fire so continuously that cartridges stuck in the overheated guns. At other moments, they held their fire for a while—then sent a volley into the Indian force when they thought it again began to move up the hill.

June 26 was another day of sun beating down on the exposed soldiers. Indian warriors did not feel a need to charge the soldiers because, as Gall said, lack of water would eventually drive them down. The troopers sucked on pebbles to try to make their mouths water, and the cooks passed out raw potatoes for them to eat.

Finally, Dr. Porter demanded water for the wounded. Benteen organized soldier and packer volunteers who took what containers were available and charged six hundred feet down a ravine to the Little Bighorn, driving away four warriors in the process. Benteen's four best sharpshooters—a private, a sergeant, a blacksmith, and a saddler—sent covering fire into the bushes across the river. At least one of the men was seen dunking his face into the water along with the containers in each hand, drinking while they filled. Numerous bullets pinging the water somehow all missed him.

The trek for water cost one man's life and left seven wounded, Private Michael Madden so badly that his leg had to be amputated below the knee. Nineteen of the water collectors (not including Madden) earned Congressional Medals of Honor, the only ones awarded in this battle.

"We had a few cans of tomatoes among our stores also," Captain Varnum recalled. "These and the water was [sic] mostly consumed by the wounded" (Carroll, p. 71).

In the early afternoon, Indian firing again slowed down and, as the hours passed, nearly stopped. The village became hidden by the smoke of a big fire; behind the smokescreen, lodges were being taken down and belongings packed. Close to sunset, Benteen recalled, the village began to move out. Its orderly three-mile-long line—Northern Cheyennes leading and Hunkpapas in the rear—was still leaving the Little Bighorn when full darkness fell. Lieutenant Edgerly said the huge horse herd looked like "a great brown carpet being dragged over the ground" below (Stewart, p. 426).

Low Dog explained how, on that second day,

*we fought Reno and his forces again and killed many of them. Then the chiefs said these men had been punished enough, and that we ought to be merciful and let them go. Then we heard that another force was coming up the river...The chiefs and wise men counseled that we had fought enough and that we should not fight unless attacked. So we took our women and children and went away (Viola, p. 68).*

As darkness fell, those who had died on the hilltop were buried in a common grave. Reno's and Benteen's men cautiously came down from Reno Hill to let their horses drink and graze. The cooks made coffee and put together a meal of what rations they had. Everyone moved a little way downriver to escape the smell of dead men and animals, finding a spot where they could see in all directions. Lieutenant DeRudio and the other troopers and scouts who had spent the last day and a half in that grove of trees finally rejoined their comrades. The men slept with their guns almost in hand, afraid that they had fallen for an Indian trap, but awoke alive and somewhat rested on June 27.

The big village moved quickly south, stopping only to sleep at night, until they reached where the Hunkpapa village had been three months before, when Crazy Horse's people and the Northern Cheyennes joined it. The people rested for four days while the chiefs counseled together, finally deciding it was best now to break into their original groups. Many of the reservation residents had already left for home.

## Terry Arrives

General Terry's command had moved upstream on the Bighorn and turned up the Little Bighorn without incident. On June 27 they set off at 7:00 A.M., and Lieutenant Bradley took the scouts ahead to the hills on the left. The main command reached the former village's northern end, where the Cheyenne lodge circle had been, and found the grass burned off, except on the moist riverbank, from the smokescreen fire. Some dogs and horses that had belonged to the Indians wandered around.

The troopers cautiously guided their horses forward past burial tipis, coming upon several beheaded and mutilated bodies of white men and then the heads of three whites hanging from a lodgepole, hair burned away, unrecognizable. Articles of soldiers' clothing lay all around, bloodstained and bullet-pierced.

At about 9:00 A.M., Bradley rode in, approached his commanders, and worked to control his voice as he said, "I have a very sad report to make. I have counted one hundred ninety-seven bodies lying in the hills." He thought he had recognized Custer, whom he had seen only in photographs (Stewart, p. 466). Terry rushed the men forward to the Little Bighorn's west bank, seeking survivors and heedlessly raising a dust cloud. From atop Reno Hill, the men first thought the cloud hid new or returning Indian warriors, but Lieutenant Varnum and Captain French raised their field glasses and announced that these were soldiers. They could see no gray horses, though, so it had to be Terry rather than Custer. Reno sent Arikara scouts Forked Horn and Young Hawk, then 2nd Lieutenant Luther Hare and 2nd Lieutenant George Wallace, with messages for his general.

As soon as the commands were reunited, Terry sent men out to search for survivors who were wounded or still hiding, and he set up camp at the site of present-day Garryowen. Dr. Porter supervised other troopers carrying the fifty-four wounded men down from Reno Hill on blanket stretchers to a field hospital he stocked from Terry's supplies. Terry ordered Captain Edward Ball of the Montana Column and his company to follow the village's trail. They would return after seeing that it forked at the Bighorn Mountains. The general also sent privates Bostwick and Goodwin to alert Grant Marsh to prepare the *Far West* for transporting wounded men. When the boat was not where it should be at the mouth of the Little Bighorn, they logically headed down the Bighorn, thinking it was hung up on rocks in the shallow river, and trekked all the way to the Yellowstone. They did not know that Captain Baker had ordered the *Far West* past the Little Bighorn and even farther upstream on the Bighorn.

The search parties began by following the tracks of Custer's uphill retreat. They found Calhoun's company and then Keogh's on the way to the top. They shot the wounded horses, except for the one recognized as Captain Keogh's mount, Comanche, which was treated and would be taken back to Fort Abraham Lincoln. In later years, a poignant but false legend claimed that he was Custer's horse and had been the lone living being on the battleground, standing by his master's body. Comanche would live out his days as a revered mascot on cavalry posts. After his death in 1891, the body was preserved and is still on exhibit at University of Kansas, in Lawrence, wearing a cavalry saddle. After the army sent Comanche there for taxidermy, it never reclaimed him.

On June 28, the scouts were sent farther afield in case they could find any soldiers who had escaped the battle, but they did not. Around the battlefield, burial details went to work with the few available tools. Among them was Lieutenant Edward J. McClernand of the Second Cavalry, who would write, "As we had but a few spades, the burial of the dead was more of a pretense than reality. A number were simply covered with sage brush [sic]. Yet we did our best" (McClernand, p. 94).

Historian John Gray believes the total army dead on the Little Bighorn, including Custer's approximately 215 men, was 263; not all bodies found could be identified. When the command finally pulled away from the battlefield, a dozen of the wounded men were able to ride horseback. Each of the forty other surviving wounded men was on a blanket litter carried by eight others. Crow scouts placed White Swan on a travois. The going was slow, with all the wounded but White Swan suffering greatly as they were jostled along. If the Indian warriors returned, half of Terry's command would be holding a litter.

Terry ordered a halt so that uninjured troopers could weave rawhide litters the next day, hanging each hammock between two horses and topping it with a buffalo robe. At 6:00 P.M. on June 29, they pulled out again, reaching the steamboat in a rainstorm at about two o'clock in the morning on June 30.

## Aboard Far West

The scout Curley was the first man to reach the *Far West* with news of the cavalry loss, having traveled two and a half days and reaching the boat the same day it arrived at the Little Bighorn's mouth. With no Crow speakers and no interpreter, however, Grant Marsh and his crew could not understand the teenager completely as he struggled with hand gestures and sketches to tell the story. They figured out that a battle had occurred, but not how it ended until the next day, June 29, when Muggins Taylor arrived en route to Fort Ellis.

Some of Custer's Arikara scouts, who made it to Terry's Powder River base camp, faced the same language barrier. Major Orlando Moore

*Indian scouts who were with Custer at the Battle of the Little Bighorn visit Little Bighorn Battlefield, 1933.*

COURTESY DENVER PUBLIC LIBRARY, WESTERN HISTORY COLLECTION, RICHARD THROSSEL PHOTO, X-31546.

and his men spent a few days thinking the cavalry had won the battle.

As soon as Terry's command reached the *Far West*, the wounded were put aboard and laid on the deck. Supplies were unloaded for Gibbon's command and the seven surviving companies of Seventh Cavalry, who were to march to base camp. A day was spent filling the boat with wood for fuel. General Terry sent Muggins Taylor to carry his official dispatch to Fort Ellis. The exhausted scout made it only partway and collapsed at a Stillwater River ranch whose owner continued in his place. Rancher Horace Countryman found the telegraph wires down at Fort Ellis and Bozeman, so he rode many miles farther north to Helena. Arriving on the Fourth of July, he persuaded a newspaper office to telegraph General Sheridan in Chicago.

On July 1 the boat left, taking General Terry, his staff, Major Brisbin, and the Gatling gun crew to Fort Pease. By the time the *Far West* had traveled fifty-three miles on the Bighorn, it was late afternoon on July 2. The officers disembarked to await their men, who soon marched in under Gibbon's command.

From July 3 through 5, Grant Marsh pushed his steamboat down the Yellowstone and then the Missouri so fast his record would never be broken: 710 miles from the mouth of the Bighorn to Bismarck in fifty-four hours, with stops. Another trooper died on board; Private William George was buried at the mouth of the Powder River. Marsh stopped briefly at Fort Stevenson in Dakota Territory for black cloth to drape the boat's superstructure and lowered the flag to half-mast before reaching Bismarck on the night of the July 5. After a brief stop, the boat moved on to Fort Abraham Lincoln.

While the nation learned of the army's defeat, General Crook was leading a big-game hunting party into the Wyoming part of the Bighorn Mountains during the first ten days of July. The Crow scouts headed home, only to discover that their reservation had received no rations so far that summer, and the Arikaras moved to their old Powder River base camp. Back east, the top brass began planning their next move. The victors separated into their tribal groups and went about their daily life of hunting, tanning hides, and preserving food for the next winter. But their triumph at the Battle of the Little Bighorn had not ended the Great Sioux War.

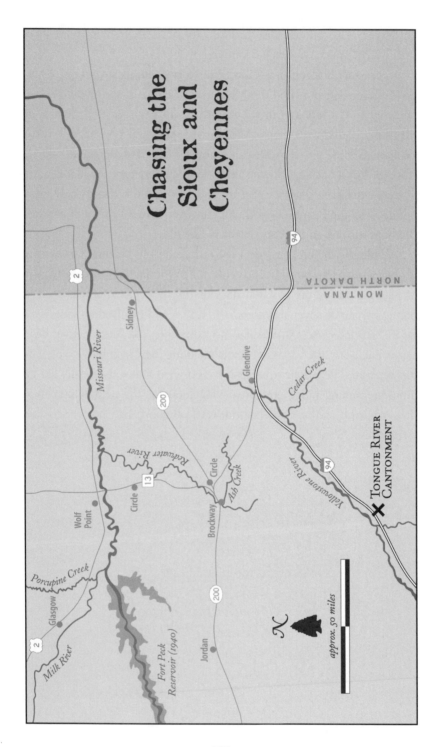

Chasing the Sioux and Cheyennes

MONTANA | NORTH DAKOTA

Milk River
Glasgow
2
Porcupine Creek
Wolf Point
Missouri River
Sidney
2
Fort Peck Reservoir (1940)
Cirdle
13
Redwater River
200
Jordan
200
Brockway
Ash Creek
Cirdle
Glendive
Cedar Creek
94
Yellowstone River
94
TONGUE RIVER
CANTONMENT
✕

approx. 50 miles

130

# CEDAR CREEK
# AND ASH CREEK
# — 1876 —

Montana would see three more battles of the Great Sioux War, but the white people eventually won by attrition rather than military might. Immediately after the Battle of the Little Bighorn, the army began pouring troops into the area, reinforcing General George Crook's men in Wyoming and General Alfred Terry's combined Montana and Dakota columns in Montana.

Terry's command spent two months preparing and then looking for the big village of Sioux, Northern Cheyennes, and other nontreaty and summer-hunting Indians. Terry exhausted his men riding and marching around southeastern Montana, commandeered steamboats for army use and ran them up and down the Yellowstone, and used up tons of supplies. He never learned that the village's tribes and bands had separated, each one going its own way to hunt and avoid soldiers.

Colonel Nelson A. Miles, assigned to a new fort on the Yellowstone River, would change things that autumn.

## Preparing and Preparing

Crook stayed in Wyoming for the entire month of July 1876, while he waited for reinforcements. He at last contacted Terry in Montana. In mid-July, couriers from Terry found Crook and returned Crook's reply at the beginning of August. Each general promised to cooperate with the other. Crook, who was not sending out scouts, believed the non-treaty Indians were in the Bighorn Mountains in Wyoming. Terry, he said, should move in that direction and Crook would meet him when his added troops arrived, but he did not say where or when.

Crook revealed his frustration when he wrote to General Sheridan on July 23. Colonel Wesley Merritt's reinforcing Fifth Cavalry had not yet arrived, and Crook claimed his inaction was embarrassing, but necessary for such an outnumbered command.

In Montana, Terry was learning how shallow the prairie rivers became as summer progressed and snowmelt stopped. Even Grant Marsh could no longer push a steamboat up the Bighorn River, and worried about getting up the Yellowstone River as far as the Fort Pease base camp. Terry therefore moved his base again, east and down the Yellowstone, across from the mouth of Rosebud Creek and today's Forsyth. Troops arrived there on July 30. Terry continued to depend on the *Far West* and several other steamboats until early September.

"Fort Beans" is what the troopers promptly named their new camp—a punning reference to the dietary staple there, and to the familiar trading post Fort Pease and the military Fort Rice in Dakota Territory. In case of Sioux and Northern Cheyenne attack, the general had the men build earthen barricades, but Fort Beans would be abandoned late that August.

Two days later the steamboat *Carroll* arrived with six companies of the Twenty-second Infantry under Colonel Elwell S. Otis. The following day, August 2, the *E. H. Durfee* brought Colonel Nelson A. Miles and his six companies of the Fifth Infantry, and the *Josephine* delivered supplies, recruits, and replacement cavalry horses, or "remounts."

Miles, a Civil War general of volunteers who would seek the regular army rank of general until late in his career, was married to a niece of General of the Army William Tecumseh Sherman. He freely wrote personal letters of information, suggestions, and requests to "Uncle Cump"—which the older soldier just as freely ignored. Colonel Miles, besides considering Colonel Custer a friend, was eager to fight Indians and had not personally experienced any defeats as Crook and Terry had. And, as fellow officers acknowledged, Miles was an ambitious officer working to overcome his disadvantage of not having attended West Point. He would succeed in becoming Commanding General of the Army in 1895, holding the post until retirement in 1903.

In another week, General Terry took his much enlarged command

132

back into the field, heading up Rosebud Creek to find the Indian village. Captain Louis Sanger, two companies of the Seventeenth Infantry, an artillery battery, and 120 cavalry recruits manned Fort Beans. With Terry went seventeen hundred men in eleven cavalry and twenty-one infantry companies, seventy-five Crow and Arikara scouts, and 240 supply wagons.

A huge column of dust appeared ahead on August 10, and Terry prepared to attack. Instead of Indians this time it was Crook's column. Here were nearly 2,300 men, 1,800 of them soldiers, and 250 of them Indian scouts and warriors. Among the four army-supplied scouts was Buffalo Bill Cody. Newspapers sent along three reporters to wire dispatches for national distribution, reflecting continuing national interest six weeks after the Battle of the Little Bighorn.

## Pointless Searches

The combined force took minimal rations and went east to the Tongue River, then farther east to explore the Powder River and its tributaries. All the Indian trails they found were old. For four of the thirteen days that the army marched, unseasonably cold rain drenched the area. Men got sick, officers disagreed on where to go and stopped speaking to each other, and no nontreaty village was found. Terry returned to his base without meeting up with Crook.

Colonel Miles removed his six infantry companies from the scout on August 10. Terry agreed when Miles suggested that his men return north to the Yellowstone and patrol to prevent Indians from escaping that way. Using the *Far West*, Miles stationed a company each on the Yellowstone, the mouth of the Tongue River and at the Powder River, and stayed aboard while the steamboat searched farther north down the Yellowstone. Soon, as the generals moved east, Miles would close the camp at the Tongue River and send its men to the Powder, at the site of his namesake, present-day Miles City.

A week after Miles left, Terry's and Crook's full command arrived at the Powder River camp, near today's town of Terry. The temporary camp had nowhere near enough rations for all the men, whose moods worsened even while they got a week of rest. The two generals were by

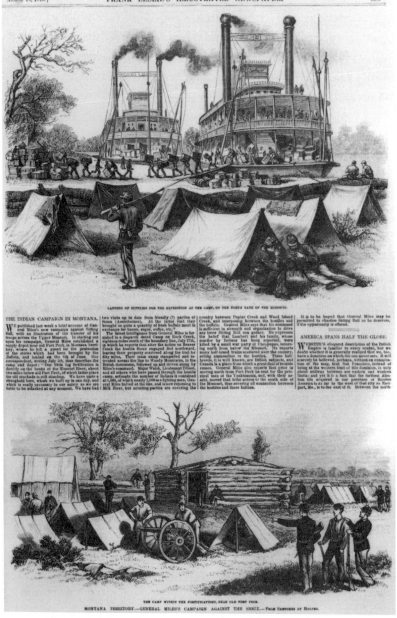

*These 1879 scenes show an army bivouac, with the steamboat* Dakota *on call. In the era's tradition, Col. Miles is referred to as "general," his highest Civil War rank.*

now communicating only through notes. Reports from Arikara scouts who had found old trails east of the lower Yellowstone convinced Terry he should go that way. (Just before reaching today's Miles City, the Yellowstone bends from west–east to southwest–northeast.) At last, on August 22, supply wagons from Fort Beans arrived with shoes that Crook's command badly needed, plus rations and forage.

Tired of being sent to scout only old trails, both the Shoshones with Crook and the Crows with Terry decided they had had enough and left for home on August 20. Reporters' dispatches and officers' and enlisted men's conversations, diaries, and letters home complained about how the two generals had accomplished nothing for two whole months since Custer died. Miles wrote his wife how demoralized the commands were. Lt. Col. Eugene Carr, of Crook's command, wrote his wife that the men were being "kept out and exposed because two fools do not know their business. I would leave the expedition today, if I could" (Gray, p. 228).

When the *Carroll* left to evacuate eighty-four ailing men to Fort Buford on August 23, two bored reporters and Cody were also aboard, but they would not get away so easily. The boat soon met the *Josephine* heading upstream and learned that Indian gunfire recently had killed a deck guard on the steamer *Yellowstone* while it traveled the Missouri River. The *Carroll*'s captain turned around and went back to the Powder; the invalids would not reach Fort Buford on the Missouri until August 29.

Terry arrived at the Powder River on August 22, anxious to lead the great command up that stream and then east to locate the big village. Intending to refine plans with Crook the next day, Terry did not find the junior general's command at the mouth of the Power. Terry began leading his men up the Power to catch up. After having marched for three days, Terry still had not met Crook.

The generals' reunion was not to be. First Terry received a courier-delivered dispatch about the attack on the steamer *Yellowstone*, and then came orders from General Philip Sheridan. Terry was to build a cantonment, or temporary fort, on the Yellowstone River at the mouth of the Tongue. Winter supplies for fifteen hundred men would soon be arriving by steamboat. Colonel Miles would command the cantonment, and Terry was to return to St. Paul headquarters by October 15.

Gibbon's Montana Column was to return to its forts and the Seventh Cavalry to Fort Abraham Lincoln.

Terry at once ordered his men back to the Yellowstone, sending a small party up the Powder River to inform Crook. Then Terry returned to the Yellowstone by boat to deal with building a fort. As soon as he had given orders to the *Yellowstone* and *Carroll* to go down the Yellowstone River for the expected building materials, Terry took troops and a pack train for a quick search north of Glendive Creek. Terry also ordered Major Marcus A. Reno and the Seventh Cavalry to check Yellowstone crossings as far north as Fort Buford on the Missouri. As before the Little Bighorn battle, Reno cut his mission short. He marched only thirty miles beyond Glendive Creek but reported all was clear as far as Fort Buford.

Crook headed east along the path of the Dakota Column's wagon trail from the previous June, apparently believing that it would lead to a more recent Indian trail. Crook soon had left Montana Territory behind.

That same August, a new law tied the Sioux's annuities to their staying on the Great Sioux Reservation, banning any Indian who hunted in the unceded lands from receiving food and supplies. Going out to hunt, even during the summer, meant losing all benefits for the rest of the year. Beginning in September, white men whom the Indians called "peace talkers" toured villages arguing the advantages of education, farming, and living in reservation houses versus being harassed by soldiers.

On September 5, General Terry finally declared the 1876 summer campaign ended. In trying to drive Indians from the unceded lands, the army had netted defeats on Rosebud Creek and the Little Bighorn River, and at the very best a draw on the Powder River, its major battles. Some, but not all, of the nontreaty Indians had decided to move onto the reservation.

By then, Two Moon's Northern Cheyennes were traveling between the Tongue River and Rosebud Creek, hunting and drying meat. Crazy Horse's Oglala Sioux village moved into present-day western North Dakota. Dull Knife's larger group of Northern Cheyennes prepared their winter supplies on the Powder River. Sitting Bull and his Hunkpapa Sioux pulled their travois northeast onto hunting land east of the Yellowstone River and south of today's Glendive.

## Army Victory at Slim Buttes

Meanwhile, General Crook's troops searched for nontreaty Indians outside of future Montana. Having found none, and running low on supplies, Crook began moving toward the Black Hills mining camps. There he planned to resupply before returning to the field.

On September 5, one more in a series of rainy days, Crook sent Capt. Anson Mills and some men ahead to bring back supplies for the main command. Four days later, Mills came upon a small Sioux village at Slim Buttes in future northwestern South Dakota.

As Mills attacked at 9 A.M., the Sioux rushed with their families to surrounding buttes and fired down into the lodges. They also sent couriers to nearby Sioux camps for reinforcements. Mills's men gathered food, guns, and ammunition—and items taken from soldiers at the Little Bighorn—before destroying the village.

By noon, both Crook's main command and the Sioux from other villages had arrived. With about 2,000 troops against 800 warriors, Crook carried the day. The battle was the army's first victory after Little Bighorn and is considered to have turned the tide against the Sioux and Northern Cheyenne—that is, along with Nelson Miles's ongoing efforts in Montana.

## Battle of Cedar Creek

As autumn came on, Colonel Miles commanded more than one thousand troops from the Fifth, Seventeenth, and Twenty-Second Infantries at the Tongue River Cantonment, and he believed in the inadvisability of winter campaigns. By now, even General Sheridan had been convinced of that. Miles was determined to drive the last nontreaty bands onto the reservation before winter. Like the rest of the army leaders, he thought that Sitting Bull was the most important leader to defeat.

Sitting Bull's men left on their usual autumn hunt. Three times in mid-October, they shot at wagons carrying supplies up the new trail the army was wearing to the Tongue River Cantonment. Miles quickly responded, leading ten infantry companies to upper Cedar Creek, sixty-some miles east and slightly south of Glendive. On October 20, he found Sitting Bull's village of about three hundred Hunkpapa,

Minneconjou, and Sans Arc Sioux. The Sioux leader agreed to meet with Miles, which he did that day and the next. Negotiators (including Gall), mixed-blood translator John Bruguier, and aides sat on a buffalo robe out in the open, Sitting Bull wrapped in a buffalo robe against the autumn wind and Miles in a bear-fur–trimmed overcoat. (This was the Indians' first meeting with Nelson Miles, whom they called "Bear Coat" afterward.) Miles placed one company, with artillery, atop an overlooking hill, and Indian warriors watched from other hilltops and on the flats.

*Nelson A. Miles, 1876. Photograph by L. A. Huffman.* COURTESY MONTANA HISTORICAL SOCIETY.

Sitting Bull demanded that the soldiers leave the unceded lands and abandon the new trail to the Tongue River Cantonment. He said again and again that he and his people wanted to be left alone and had no desire to fight the soldiers. Miles, with the new annuities law behind him, was just as inflexible. The colonel continuously demanded that Sitting Bull explain the opinions that American newspapers recently had attributed to him, bloodthirsty predictions that the Sioux would kill all whites. Of course, no reporter had interviewed Sitting Bull, and he had no idea what Miles was talking about. And Miles demanded that the Indians surrender now and begin moving to the Great Sioux Reservation. The two-day council naturally did not resolve anything.

After talks ended on October 21, Miles ordered his troops into skirmish lines in the valley and had them move onto the hilltops, pushing the Sioux away. Fighting did not start until Miles's scouts spotted some Sioux setting the prairie afire and shot at them. The field artillery began to fire and the soldiers pushed forward, toward the lodges. The Little Bighorn battle was foremost in the soldiers' minds and, as trumpeter Edwin M. Brown recalled, "many a strong heart grew weak as our thoughts flew back" to that battle (Greene, *Yellowstone Command*, p. 103).

Smoke from the grass fire filled the air, Sioux warriors rode in and out of hiding places among the hills, and as Brown said, "bullets whistled lively over our head and around us" (Greene, *Yellowstone Command*, p. 103) as the infantry advanced with the help of artillery fire. In the bad visibility, only two soldiers and one or two Sioux were wounded, and possibly one Sioux died. The Indians abandoned their lodges and moved away, with Miles's troops following them throughout the day of October 22.

Losing their lodges, food, and other belongings was a harsh blow. Sitting Bull and thirty families escaped north toward the Missouri River, soon to be joined by Gall and others in a village of about four hundred people. Some groups went directly to the reservation, and on October 27 about two thousand Sioux surrendered and began moving to the reservation. Many of them had lived there in previous winters so were simply returning—but now with rations that Miles distributed in the field.

The battle's main result was to lessen Sitting Bull's power among the Sioux. During the two-day council, Miles became aware that not all the Sioux leaders agreed with Sitting Bull's firm stand. His leaving Cedar Creek angered some of the other leaders and helped lead to their surrenders. Although Sitting Bull would not go onto the reservation until 1881, and remained a leader respected by the Sioux and feared by the army until his death in 1890, he never again held as much power as he had in 1876.

## Battle of Ash Creek

Returning to Tongue River Cantonment, Colonel Miles stayed long enough to request that the army send warm clothing to the flimsy fort, while keeping a tough schedule of day-long field maneuvers. For six weeks, from November 6 to December 14, he led most of his command to look for Sitting Bull's village. They marched north to Fort Peck on the Missouri, then Miles took six companies southwest toward the village's rumored location near Black Buttes. Miles sent four companies under Captain Simon Snyder to move up the Big Dry River and push the village toward him. Deep snow, frigid cold, lack of forage and rations, and ice floes in the Missouri that Miles's men needed to recross doomed this plan while the village moved away from the soldiers.

When Miles learned, at the end of November, that Sitting Bull's village was now closer to Fort Peck, he assigned trusted 1st Lieutenant Frank D. Baldwin to search for it. A Civil War veteran and two-time Congressional Medal of Honor recipient who would achieve the rank of general, Baldwin took 112 men and a mule pack train east on December 2, moving along the Missouri River's north side. They stopped at Fort Peck for news on December 6, then picked up the village's recent trail that same day near the mouth of Porcupine Creek on the Milk River.

Baldwin caught up with the village on December 7, just as it was crossing the frozen Missouri near Bark Creek. Soldiers and Sioux fired at each other across the ice, but the army withdrew, Baldwin's subordinate officers agreeing they held a bad position against the estimated six hundred Sioux warriors. A blizzard forced the infantry back to Fort Peck, two more days of marching that left the men exhausted and a fourth of them frostbitten.

Sitting Bull sent a messenger to Fort Peck warning that he would attack the command when it tried to move back to Tongue River Cantonment and that he would also attack Fort Peck. Baldwin notified Miles that he intended to drive the village south to the Yellowstone, where Miles could attack.

Leaving Fort Peck on December 11 with the men riding in wagons, Baldwin's command resupplied at Wolf Point Agency. The Missouri's ice held as they carefully pulled the unhitched wagons across on December 14. By then the soldiers were wrapping buffalo hides around what remained of their shoes. They moved south and into the Redwater River valley, and on December 18 began following its tributary, Ash Creek, upstream through the snow.

That afternoon Baldwin found Sitting Bull's camp in the area east of present-day Brockway, marched to it in battle formation, and attacked. Although the village now contained 122 lodges, its warriors were away hunting. As soon as the battalion's howitzer began firing, the Hunkpapa

*Artist Charles Holtes pictures what a winter campaign in Montana was like.*
COURTESY DENVER PUBLIC LIBRARY, WESTERN HISTORY COLLECTION, PHOTOGRAPHIC REPRODUCTION OF ILLUSTRATIONS BY HOLTES IN *FRANK LESLIE'S ILLUSTRATED NEWS*, 1880, X-33623.

Sioux in the village abandoned their homes and rode south, where they found help and shelter at an Oglala village. They soon began to move north again and early the next year crossed the border into Canada, hoping for better treatment from "Grandmother's" (Queen Victoria's) soldiers.

Baldwin's Fifth Infantry let them go, capturing ponies and mules left behind, taking dried meat and buffalo robes for their own use, and burning the rest. Baldwin claimed that one Indian was killed, but none of his men was wounded in the battle or during sniping at their nearby camp that night. Sioux following the command after it reached the Yellowstone en route to Tongue River Cantonment attacked, but were quickly repulsed.

By the time they reached their fort on December 22, Baldwin's men had marched more than seven hundred miles, even more than the five-hundred–plus of Miles's men during November and December. The command's persistence under severe winter conditions impressed nontreaty Indians as the news spread.

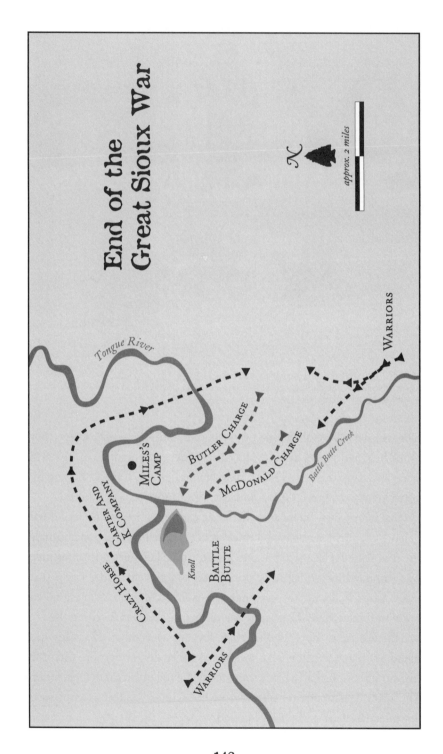

# End of the
# Great Sioux War

Tongue River

Miles's Camp

Butler Charge

McDonald Charge

Battle Butte Creek

Carter and K Company

Crazy Horse

Knoll

Battle Butte

Warriors

Warriors

*N*

*approx. 2 miles*

# BATTLE OF
# WOLF MOUNTAINS
# — 1877 —

After they had weakened Sitting Bull and his people, the U.S. Army in early 1877 began to focus on Crazy Horse and his village. Over the months since separating after the Battle of the Little Bighorn, many lodges had rejoined Crazy Horse's Oglala Sioux village. They included other nontreaty Sioux, Two Moon's Northern Cheyennes, and Sioux leaving the reservation because of the Black Hills controversy and lack of food. By late November, the village held about 250 lodges, and soon welcomed as many as 500 more Sioux lodges. It stayed below the Yellowstone River in southeastern Montana and northern Wyoming, the Indians hunting on the upper waters of Rosebud Creek, the Tongue River, and the Powder River.

In Wyoming during November 1876, General Crook sent Colonel Ranald Mackenzie looking for Crazy Horse. His cavalry instead found Dull Knife's Northern Cheyennes in the Wyoming portion of the Bighorn Mountains and attacked them on November 25. Soldiers destroyed the village, wounded many Cheyennes, and killed as many as forty of them. Most of the Cheyennes escaped and headed north without warm clothing, food, or shelter. Many adults and children froze to death marching through the snow, but by early December the survivors had joined Crazy Horse's village on the Tongue River in Montana. Now the village numbered nearly eight hundred lodges.

An early winter, scarce game, and the added burden of Dull Knife's impoverished people convinced the leaders to send five men and a few warriors to Tongue River Cantonment to meet with Miles and discuss surrender. Even Crazy Horse agreed. An Oglala chief named Sitting Bull (not the Hunkpapa leader) led the mission. He got along well with whites but had left the Great Sioux Reservation because of the Black Hills situation. Mackenzie's attack on Dull Knife's Northern Cheyennes then strengthened his belief that making peace was necessary.

On December 16, five men approached the fort showing two truce flags and leaving the accompanying warriors behind. They first reached the riverbank encampment of newly recruited Crow scouts, their traditional enemies. The Crows ignored their peaceful greeting and murdered them on the spot. Miles—just back from his six weeks in the field—fired the Crows in anger over their destroying a chance to shorten the war. He also tried but failed to contact Crazy Horse and explain what had happened.

For Crazy Horse and other leaders in the village, that was the end of talking peace. Crazy Horse soon organized a series of raids on the fort, its beef herd, and its mail couriers, hoping to draw the cavalry out and ambush it. Going generally southwest along the Tongue River, the Sioux and Cheyennes left obvious signs of camps, kept small to delude army scouts about their strength. About one hundred warriors formed this group of decoys.

Miles responded as Crazy Horse had hoped, leaving Tongue River Cantonment on December 29, only a week after Lieutenant Frank D. Baldwin's men had returned from Ash Creek. The battalion contained 436 officers and enlisted men (mostly the Fifth Infantry and some Twenty-Second Infantry), field artillery, and supply wagons. Along with five Indian scouts, Miles took Luther "Yellowstone" Kelly and John "Liver-Eating" Johnson, Thomas H. LeForge (whose broken collarbone had kept him from the Little Bighorn battle), James Parker, and George Johnson. Men and wagons slogged up the Tongue River through deep snow in subzero temperatures. For ten days they marched, huddling in bulky buffalo and blanket coats and getting soaked in frigid water when wagons broke through the ice as they crossed and recrossed the winding river. Even though Miles hurried his men along, he soon ordered that a fire be kindled at each river crossing to prevent them from freezing to death.

On January 7, in new snow left by a blizzard that had blown the entire previous day, the battalion reached a three-hundred-foot-wide floodplain below what is now called Battle Butte, a few miles southwest of today's Birney. Here at the Wolf Mountains' northern end, Miles had unknowingly stopped a couple of miles downstream from Prairie Dog Creek, where Crazy Horse had planned his ambush. Just a few miles on the other side of the Wolf Mountains was the site of the Battle of Rosebud Creek.

Colonel Miles made it a short day and set up camp in cottonwood trees that filled a northward horseshoe bend of the Tongue. The dry bed of Battle Butte Creek was four hundred yards from camp. He sent Captain Ezra P. Ewers and Company E of the Fifth Infantry, with artillery, up a conical hill between the camp and Battle Butte. The hill's west side was a cliff, making it easier to defend. Ewers's men built breastworks on a spot overlooking camp and the approach from the direction of the Indians' trail.

Below and north of them, 1st Lieutenant Mason Carter and Company K were sent across the frozen Tongue River to guard against attack from the hills north of camp. They dug in amid a grove of cottonwoods.

Miles's Crow scouts reported enemy warriors south of camp. The army scouts went out to survey the surrounding area, soon finding four Northern Cheyenne women and their children returning home from visiting relatives. Big Horn, a warrior with them who had been away on his own scout, glimpsed the white men capturing the women and children. Believing that the prisoners would be killed, he raced to find the Crazy Horse–Two Moon village and shout his news. The chiefs gathered their warriors and set out to attack the infantry camp, the Sioux from its west and the Cheyennes from its north.

After escorting the women to camp, the five white scouts went out again as darkness neared. They were attacked by the Indian decoy party, who were pretending to inspect where the Cheyenne women had been captured. This party had created its own ambush a mile from the army camp, leaving a few men visible while most of them hid. Springing out, they surprised the scouts, who foolishly attacked. Warriors killed two of the scouts' horses and sent a bullet zinging alongside Johnson's head that took a chunk of his shaggy hair.

While the white scouts barricaded themselves in nearby trees,

Miles's command formed lines to defend their camp. His Indian scouts moved to aid Kelly's men in the trees. Miles sent Captain James S. Casey and Company A across the Tongue and up a hill with an artillery piece, reinforced by 2nd Lieutenant Charles E. Hargous and mounted infantry to rescue the scouts. More warriors joined the scouts' attackers, doubling their number, and fired into the soldiers for about an hour until the artillery drove the Indians away. The soldiers returned to camp with the scouts, and the men got what rest they could.

While three new feet of snow fell overnight, the main body of Northern Cheyennes and Sioux moved into their attack positions. They apparently did not know about the decoy party's fight and expected to surprise the soldiers when dawn came. Occasional firing into Miles's camp overnight apparently came from the decoys. In the morning, snow was still falling while Miles and his men had breakfast.

## Threat of a Surround

The Crow scouts galloped into the camp to announce that Sioux and Cheyenne warriors were approaching. Colonel Miles climbed to Ewers's emplacement and spotted an estimated six hundred warriors. His immediate concern was to prevent them from surrounding the camp from atop the bluffs and hills. He deployed men to the south and east and went with more men and artillery pieces to reinforce Ewers. To the left of Company K's entrenchment in the trees but across the Tongue on the camp side, he placed Companies E and F of the Twenty-Second. Teamsters hid the mules between the wagons and lay freezing in the snow for protection during the fight.

At 7:00 A.M. on January 8, amid falling snow, the main body of Sioux and Cheyennes began attacking. Blowing their eagle-bone whistles, they fired into empty army tents in hopes the men were still sleeping. The Cheyenne chief Medicine Bear led a charge down the Tongue's west bank to attack Ewers's hilltop position. Warriors repeatedly charged Lieutenant Mason Carter and Company K on the flat and retreated into safety in ravines; the soldiers' return gunfire was supplemented by artillery fire from 1st Lieutenant James W. Pope across the Tongue behind Company K. Eventually these advances

146

stopped and the warriors stayed hidden to fire on Carter's men.

Medicine Bear led two hundred men up Battle Butte just south of Ewers's hilltop, where they could fire down on the artillery. They were soon joined by more Cheyennes with the holy man Big Crow, and Sioux with Crazy Horse who had ridden nearly full circle north, east, and south around the infantry camp to reach the spot. Ewers turned his guns in their direction, knowing he had to hold his position. At one point, a shell hit Chief Medicine Bear's horse, knocking it and its rider down but not exploding—and the chief continued fighting. Late in the morning, Miles sent Captain James S. Casey and Company A to fight their way up Battle Butte and take it from the warriors hiding among the trees and rocks. Casey promptly captured the first of three peaks, but Crazy Horse held him there. Miles sent Company D under 1st Lieutenant Robert McDonald to reinforce Company A.

The soldiers drove back the warriors on the second peak of Battle Butte's crest. Firing from just below the second peak, a soldier's bullet hit Big Crow, which seriously affected the Cheyennes' morale. Some began withdrawing after retrieving the mortally wounded holy man. When he asked to be left on the butte to die, they honored the request.

Crazy Horse and about three hundred warriors holding the crucial third peak of Battle Butte began advancing down it toward the two companies of soldiers. Seeing this, Miles sent Captain Edmund Butler and Company C charging up the ridge under heavy fire. When Butler's horse was shot, he led up the steepening hill on foot. Five hundred warriors and soldiers fired continuously at each other after Butler's men reached the top. Pope redirected his artillery fire at the third peak, aiming a three-inch gun and a Napoleon gun at the Sioux and Cheyennes, which slowly forced them back and down the hill. They continued fighting as the soldiers pushed them back for about a mile. When the snow that was still falling whirled into a blizzard, they retreated.

As the Indians moved away, the soldiers began to reunite at about noon. One soldier was dead, another mortally wounded, and seven would recover from their wounds. The Indians counted even fewer casualties, but after Miles inspected blood spots on the snowy battleground the next day, he overestimated twenty to twenty-five Indian dead.

*The Battle of Wolf Mountains, 1877.*

Miles ordered the camp moved to the top of Battle Butte, including supplies removed from the wagons, which the soldiers accomplished in blinding snow and wind. The command spent two nights on the butte while the Sioux and Northern Cheyennes traveled out of the area, to the headwaters of the Bighorn River in Wyoming's part of the Bighorn Mountains.

Leaving Battle Butte on January 10, the battalion made its way through snow for four days until another blizzard struck, further slowing the miserable march, and finally reached Tongue River Cantonment on January 18. The Great Sioux War's winter campaign had ended.

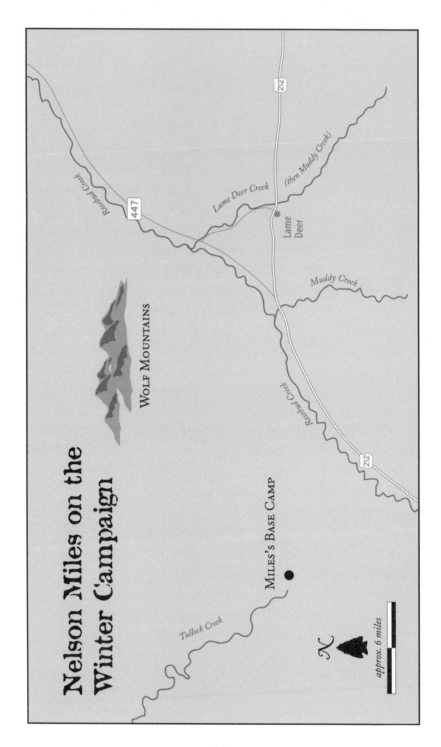

Nelson Miles on the Winter Campaign

WOLF MOUNTAINS

Rosebud Creek

447

Lame Deer Creek

(then Muddy Creek)

Lame Deer

212

Muddy Creek

Rosebud Creek

212

Tullock Creek

MILES'S BASE CAMP

N

approx. 6 miles

# BATTLE OF
# MUDDY CREEK
# — 1877 —

Minneconjou Sioux chief Lame Deer and his small village returned to the unceded land of southeastern Montana as winter faded into spring in 1877. To their sixty lodges were added fifteen more of Chief White Hawk's Northern Cheyennes, and by May the larger village was staying along a Rosebud Creek tributary then called Muddy Creek. Today its name is Lame Deer Creek in memory of what happened there, and a nearby stream is now called Muddy Creek.

More than four hundred people were hunting and living comfortably, blessed with a herd of about 450 ponies, and free of both white soldiers and the Indians willing to surrender to them. The latter, including Crazy Horse's village in May 1877, moved their lodges to Camp Robinson in Nebraska, giving in to living on the Great Sioux Reservation. Some even became army scouts, including Crazy Horse and the Northern Cheyenne called White Bull or Ice.

In February, Miles had negotiated surrender with Cheyennes and Sioux and they nearly came in to Tongue River Cantonment. But as they rode in that direction early in March, Indian messengers brought news that surrender terms were better at the reservation. In good faith, the chiefs talked again with Miles. He had little to offer, his fort having had trouble obtaining its own supplies all winter. Finally most of the bands chose the Sioux reservation, and Colonel Miles unhappily heard that General George Crook received the credit for getting them to go in. Under Two Moon and other chiefs, including some Sioux, Northern Cheyennes surrendered at the Tongue River.

With their schedule of daily drills, Miles's soldiers stayed ready to return to the field. Reinforcements and a shipment of grain for the horses arrived near the end of April, and the colonel sent his troops out in stages between April 29 and May 30. He led a battalion of 450 men and twenty-one officers of the Fifth and Twenty-second Infantries and the Second Cavalry, with Indian and white scouts, and supply wagons.

They began searching for Lame Deer's village, heading up the Tongue River and then moving west to Rosebud Creek and following it upstream. On May 5, Miles had the supply wagons form a base camp at the head of Tullock Creek, east of today's Hardin. The newly recruited scouts, who knew this country well, reported seeing the village in the distance the next day, sitting on Muddy Creek.

Miles commanded his men to pack two days' rations and prepare for a night march. They traveled southeast in a rainstorm from two o'clock to four-thirty in the morning of May 7, the soldiers on horseback soon well ahead of the infantry, and reached the sleeping village (near today's town of Lame Deer).

The attack began with cavalry and mounted infantry driving away and capturing the village's pony herd. Miles ordered his other troops to try not to shoot women and children when startled families began running out of their lodges.

As soon as the fighting started, the scouts pointed out Chief Lame Deer to Miles, who ordered his soldiers to stop shooting while he and the chief cautiously approached each other to talk. Four warriors came forward with Lame Deer, and Miles led eight soldiers and scouts. Lame Deer held his rifle, as did his nephew Iron Star.

When Miles had his interpreter order Lame Deer to put his gun down, the chief did—leaving it cocked, pointing toward Miles, and close at hand. White Bull made sure Miles knew this, then rode forward and tried to grab Iron Star's gun, which went off but didn't hit anyone.

Lame Deer at once picked up his gun, aimed at Miles, and fired, but the colonel just as quickly pulled his horse aside. His orderly, Private Charles Shrenger, instead was shot and killed. Everyone began shooting again, and Lame Deer soon lay dead. Iron Star escaped but ran right into another company of soldiers, whose commander killed him. White Bull scalped Lame Deer, his one-time ally against these same soldiers.

*Sitting Bull and Sioux band cross the Yellowstone River near Fort Keogh to surrender to General Miles.*

Warriors grabbed their favorite war ponies—always tethered nearby—and quickly moved south and up some bluffs. They sent heavy fire down on Miles's battalion, which left a company to guard the village and then attacked the ridge from right, center, and left. Private William F. Zimmer of the Second Cavalry wrote in his journal:

> *...we dismounted & clambered up the hill after the Indians. The hills were from 70 to 100 feet high & very steep. We were obliged to clamber on our hands and knees & grab on bushes for assistance to reach the top. All this time the Indians were shooting at the Co. in their camp, who were so far away that they did but little harm, and paying little or no attention to us, once in a while a bullet would whistle pretty close. (Zimmer, p. 47)*

Soldiers eventually flanked the warriors, and the fight ended before 9:00 A.M. The bodies of fourteen Indians—women included—were

*Fort Custer, 1887. Photographer unidentified.* COURTESY MONTANA HISTORICAL SOCIETY.

found on the battlefield, and the soldiers counted four dead and nine wounded. All the dead were buried there.

Soldiers burned the lodges and all their contents, including what Private Zimmer called "lots of stuff belonging to the Seventh Cavalry that they got at the Custer massacre" (Zimmer, pp. 50–51). Miles set up camp and a hospital nearby, where his infantry arrived about noon. Throughout the afternoon and night, Sioux occasionally fired into camp from the surrounding hills.

The next morning, May 8, Miles ordered his infantry to ride back to Tongue River Cantonment on the Indian ponies, which troopers found difficult to control. He had the remaining ponies shot so that surviving Sioux could not retrieve them. Leaving Muddy Creek that day, the soldiers made only eight miles' progress because of difficulties with their new mounts. Warriors tried but failed to recapture their horses that night. After that, Miles's battalion continued back to Tongue River Cantonment without incident, arriving on May 14.

The Great Sioux War was over, and most of the nontreaty Indians were now on or heading toward the reservation. By the end of 1877, a permanent post two miles away had replaced Tongue River

Cantonment and been christened Fort Keogh. The town of Miles City was platted and began life as the fort's service center. Colonel Miles's wife, daughter, and niece—whom he had not seen for a year—moved into the fort, as did the families of junior officers. The second fort that General Sherman wanted on the Yellowstone River fort was sited at the mouth of the Bighorn and named Fort Custer. Sherman himself toured the area in July 1877, reviewing troops and awarding thirty-one Congressional Medals of Honor.

# Nez Perce Trail in Montana

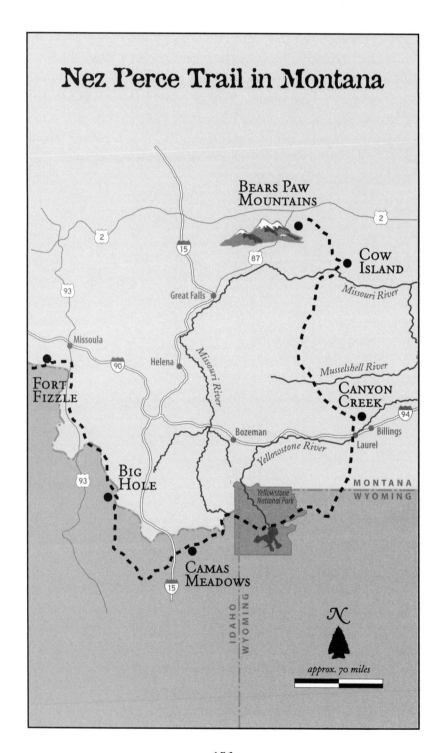

# NEZ PERCE WAR BEGINS
## — 1877 —

The Nez Perce War of 1877 was punctuated by five major battles and even more numerous smaller actions between the Indians and the U.S. Army. Five of them, including the last, occurred in Montana Territory, and the others in Idaho Territory. Montanans often refer to the event as the "Flight of the Nez Perces," because the people were on the move rather than at war, seeking to get away from the army and return to their normal lives. At first, they headed toward their longtime allies, the Crows, in southeastern Montana. Later conditions caused the Nez Perces to turn north toward Canada, as Sitting Bull's Sioux had done not so long before.

The Nez Perces traveling between June and October 1877 were not a war party, but rather families transporting their lodges and belongings and leading the village's horse herd that originally held two thousand head. Excellent horsemen who had refined the Indian-bred dappled Appaloosa breed since obtaining horses a century and a half ago, the Nez Perces fought in semi-organized formations—unlike the Sioux that the army had battled the previous year.

Less than one-third of the six hundred people who initially left Idaho (additional Nez Perces joined the trek later) were men, and an estimated one hundred or so of the men were warriors. Four bands of Nez Perces and one band of their close relatives, the Palouse Indians, made up the group. Each independent band was headed by several chiefs who governed by consensus, and all the headmen in the traveling village joined in council to make decisions.

Chiefs of the largest band were Joseph and his younger brother Ollokot. Neither was a war leader when the war began, and Joseph mostly managed the day-to-day living arrangements. (As Ollokot gained

*Chief Joseph at Bismarck, November 1877. Photograph by O. S. Goff.*

fighting experience over the coming months, he would emerge as a skilled war leader.) The other significant Nez Perce chiefs were White Bird, Looking Glass, and Toohoolhoolzote, and the Palouse chief was Husis Kute.

These people were nontreaty Nez Perces and Palouses. Chiefs of their bands had not signed the 1855 Fort Walla Walla treaty that established a reservation in their home country of southeastern Washington Territory, northeastern Oregon, and northern Idaho Territory (Greene, *Nez Perce Summer 1877*, p. 8). They had lived in that area for ten thousand years, calling themselves *Nee-Me-Poo* (accent on the second syllable), "the people," in their language. (The current theory is that French traders saw Northwest Coast people with pierced noses visiting in Nez Perce camps, and called the Nee-Me-Poo "pierced nose"—*nez percé*, today pronounced "nezz purse.") Not having signed the 1855 treaty, many Nez Perces did not consider themselves subject to it—unlike those bands whose leaders had signed. The U.S. government failed to understand Nez Perce band-by-band government and considered the nontreaty Indians as "hostiles" who broke the treaty when they refused to move onto the reservation.

That reservation had shrunk since the first treaty, beginning when gold strikes brought white prospectors and settlers into Nez Perce country in the early 1860s. By the time of the 1863 treaty, the reservation was entirely in Idaho, east of present-day Lewiston, with agencies at Fort Lapwai and Kamiah. Joseph and his band continued to live in Oregon's Wallowa Valley, now no longer part of the reservation, but closed to white settlement by order of President Ulysses S. Grant in 1873. Whites, however, still continued to settle in the valley, and only two years later Grant rescinded his order. During the two decades since the first treaty in 1855, a total of twenty-five Nez Perces had been murdered—most of them over land disputes. Local law enforcement never prosecuted the white killers.

In 1876, a commission visited Fort Lapwai to study the problem. Among its members was General Oliver O. Howard, a Civil War veteran who had lost his right arm in the Battle of Fair Oaks. The Nez Perces called him "Cut Arm." Howard had graduated near the top of his West Point Class of 1854, fought the Seminole Indians, and served throughout the Civil War. However, he did not become one of the greatest battlefield leaders. From his headquarters in Portland, Oregon, Howard now commanded the army's Department of the Columbia, which covered the state of Oregon, and Alaska, Washington, and Idaho territories. He was forty-six years old, a decade older than Chief Joseph.

Trying to explain the Nez Perces' deep connection to their homeland on behalf of all the nontreaty people, Chief Joseph told the commission:

> *The earth and myself are of one mind. The one who has the right to dispose of it is the one who has created it.... In it are riches given me by my ancestors, and from that time up to the present I have loved the land, was thankful it had been given me.... The right to the land was ours before the whites came among us. (Greene, Nez Perce Summer 1877, pp. 17–18)*

Ultimately the commission decided, in effect, that "the majority rules." As they saw it, most Nez Perce bands had signed the previous treaties, and so all Nez Perces had to abide by them. Now even the nontreaty people had to move onto the reservation. In January 1877, they were told to be there by April 1.

The Nez Perces managed to postpone the deadline, and General Howard was sent to enforce the move peacefully. Early in May, he ordered two companies of cavalry from Fort Walla Walla to bivouac at the western end of the Wallowa Valley, poised to push the Indians northeast toward the reservation. For ten days, Howard met with nontreaty leaders. He spent one day riding across the reservation on horseback with Joseph, Looking Glass, and White Bird, looking for good unclaimed land in Joseph's assigned area. He traveled two days with just Looking Glass and White Bird, doing the same in the area where they would live. But the general lost his patience one day when Toohoolhoolzote tried again and again to explain the Nez Perces' need to live on their own homeland. Howard angrily removed the chief from the council and had him jailed for a few days.

When the meeting ended in mid-May, Howard thought all parties had agreed that the nontreaties could have a month to collect their livestock and make the move. If they were one day late, he said, soldiers would drive them forward with no regard for their livestock, and white people could claim any lost animals. Howard returned to Portland to wait until the new deadline.

# Shore Crossing's Revenge

As June began, bands of nontreaty Nez Perces and Palouses gradually gathered at Tolo Lake on Camas Prairie, east of today's Grangeville and just south of the reservation. Here they had harvested camas root, an important part of their diet, for centuries. The area long had been a place to meet, visit, and council in the summertime. Now, some reservation Indians even came to visit.

The gathering this year was not the usual placid one. Much of the talk was about the reservation deadline, and opinions were divided on what to do. Maybe the people should split up and go in different directions, maybe they should enter the reservation on schedule or maybe they should go south of the Salmon River away from whites. Maybe they should go to Crow country in Montana, or to Canada. Anger over this recent bad treatment by whites led to talk about white murderers and rapists and how they had gone unpunished, including Lawrence Ott, who had killed Eagle Robe three years before. One of the older men taunted Eagle Robe's son Shore Crossing and his young warrior friends, asking what good Shore Crossing was, since he had not avenged his father.

Eagle Robe had had a campsite and garden on White Bird Creek. When he went there in the spring of 1874, he saw that Ott had moved his farm fence to claim Eagle Robe's place. He found Ott out plowing and tried to talk with him and, finally, frustrated by Ott's belligerence, threw some rocks at the farmer's horses. Ott shot Eagle Robe, who died a few hours later. Hoping to keep peace, Eagle Robe had forbidden Shore Crossing from seeking vengeance. Ott claimed self-defense and was not charged with murder, which was typical of how law officers handled crimes against the Nez Perces.

The older warrior's taunt caused the younger men at last to retaliate, and whites' reactions would lead to the Nez Perce War. That night, June 13, 1877, Shore Crossing, his nephew Swan Necklace, and his friend Red Moccasin Top raided several area ranches. During the next three days, at least seventeen more warriors joined them. The Nez Perces had never before gone to war against whites, but this small group's raids killed eighteen whites (including one woman and two children), wounded two women and two girls, and raped three women over four days. Shore Crossing's men also burned ranch buildings and hay supplies, destroyed or took portable property, and ran off livestock.

General Howard was waiting at Fort Lapwai to receive the non-treaty bands when news of the first day's raids arrived on June 14. He immediately arranged for more troops from Fort Walla Walla to come to the area and asked the army to send troops and supplies to Lewiston. He also wired his superior in San Francisco, General Irvin McDowell: "Think we shall make short work of it" (Greene, *Nez Perce Summer 1877*, p. 34).

Instead, the Nez Perce War would continue for the next sixteen weeks, across parts of three territories.

The first battles occurred in Idaho, beginning when the army attacked Joseph's and White Bird's camp in White Bird Canyon on June 17. Captain David Perry led more than one hundred soldiers and civilian volunteers on a thirty-six-hour forced march. When the army caught up with the village in White Bird Canyon, the Nez Perces sent men carrying a truce flag to meet the soldiers, but volunteer Arthur Chapman, a translator whom Joseph considered his friend, shot one of the emissaries. Sixty-five Nez Perce warriors fired back as the cavalry charged. Almost at once the civilians panicked and retreated, with the soldiers promptly turning and following them. Thirty-four soldiers and volunteers were killed, but no Nez Perces died. Although the Nez Perces took the soldiers' guns and ammunition, it was not their custom to strip or mutilate enemies' bodies. The next day, White Bird's band moved on, heading east toward buffalo country in Montana Territory.

The second battle forced Looking Glass's band to join the hostilities. Looking Glass, the son of a treaty signer, had so far stayed out of the situation and had told Joseph and White Bird, "You have acted like fools in murdering white men. I will have no part in these things and have nothing to do with such men.... I want to live in peace" (Greene, *Nez Perce Summer 1877*, p. 53). On July 1, his eleven lodges were camped on Clear Creek, near today's Kooskia, when General Howard sent two cavalry companies to arrest Looking Glass and his warriors for not being on the reservation. Captain Stephen G. Whipple was in command. Once again, soldiers opened fire on Nez Perce men who merely went out to ask what they wanted, and then charged into camp. People ran for safety, and one woman carrying her baby was shot and drowned while she tried to swim the creek. The soldiers captured the band's twelve hundred horses and burned everything in the village.

## Looking Glass's Village Joins

Looking Glass's people—most of them now on foot—soon found and joined White Bird and Joseph, raising the mobile village's population to about 740. The nontreaty people gained one of the better war leaders in Looking Glass after, as he said,

*I have been treated worse than a dog by the very same army that was once a friend. My father's warriors fought many battles as allies of the United States soldiers...We had friends and relations killed in fighting along with the United States troops....Now, my people, as long as I live I will never make peace with the treacherous Americans. (McDonald, p. 241)*

Before Looking Glass's band had arrived, a series of three battles occurred on July 3, 4, and 5 near Cottonwood, in Idaho Territory. On the first day, White Bird's and Joseph's warriors surrounded and killed an advance party of eleven men from Captain Whipple's command. Second Lieutenant Sevier M. Rains had been sent with ten volunteers to precisely locate the Nez Perces and report back. Warriors led by Five Wounds saw them coming and surrounded them. Among these warriors was a young man named Yellow Wolf who, beginning in 1908, told his stories of the Nez Perce War through a series of interpreters to Lucullus V. McWhorter, who recorded and published them.

Rains and his men—expecting to be relieved by Whipple and the main command—took cover in some boulders but were wiped out. Whipple had started his men forward when he heard the shooting, but stopped the charge when he saw about one hundred warriors. After exchanging fire for a while, Whipple retreated.

The next day, July 4, when Whipple's men reached and started to bury the bodies of Rains's party, warriors fired on them continuously from 1:00 to 9:00 P.M. The soldiers entrenched atop a hill and held it, with no casualties. The Nez Perces began shooting again the next morning, to cover their camp's movement away from the area. They cut off a party of seventeen volunteers under Captain Darius B. Randall that had almost succeeded in joining Whipple's command, and killed three of them while Whipple hesitated only two hundred yards away. Finally some soldiers, without orders, rescued the surviving volunteers.

After bypassing the soldiers assigned to stop the nontreaty Indians from crossing Camas Prairie, the village did exactly that. Some warriors raided and burned ranches along their way to a camp on the South Fork of the Clearwater River.

Colonel Edward McConville, with seventy-five volunteers who had traveled from Lewiston via the army's local staging center at the town of Mount Idaho, nearly caught up with the Nez Perces after dark on July 8. When he and his men camped near the South Fork, they had no idea how close they were to the natives. When they awoke in the morning to see the people only a mile away, the colonel sent a dispatch to General Howard. McConville, planning to wait for Howard, had his men dig in on a hilltop, entrenching behind rocks and filling containers with water. But one of the men accidentally fired his rifle in the afternoon on July 9. While McConville's men scrambled into their little fortification, Nez Perce warriors led by Rainbow, Five Wounds, and Ollokot charged and surrounded it.

Some of the volunteers labeled their defensive position "Fort Misery"; others called it "Misery Hill" and even "Fort McConville." Some Nez Perce warriors drove off the soldiers' horses, which Yellow Wolf said included "Good horses taken from Looking Glass when soldiers came and attacked his village. We returned them to warriors who claimed them." Other warriors began firing at Fort Misery at about 1:00 A.M. on July 10 and continued until daylight. "It was just like fireworks cutting the darkness," Yellow Wolf later recalled (McWhorter, *Yellow Wolf*, p. 79).

Late that afternoon, McConville saw that another party of volunteer forces, under Major George Shearer, was approaching—and that the Nez Perces were ready to attack. He sent out troops who managed to head off the warriors and allow Shearer and his men to reach Fort Misery. The next morning, July 11, the Nez Perces let up their guard and McConville's battalion returned to Mount Idaho on foot. They obtained horses and rode to join General Howard at once.

Howard caught up with the village on July 11 and began a two-day engagement that resulted in the campaign's first partial victory—at the cost of fourteen soldiers and four Nez Perce dead. His command of 350 soldiers now included a small complement of newspaper reporters, brought along because the nation was watching.

*Yellow Wolf.*
*No date, photographer unidentified.*
COURTESY MONTANA HISTORICAL SOCIETY.

To Shore Crossing and his friends, Howard was "the Indian Herder," Chief Joseph later said (Laughy, p. 242). They especially wanted him dead because they apparently thought this would prevent his capturing them and having them hanged. Many other warriors also hoped to kill Howard, who symbolized their being forced onto the reservation.

## Battle of the Clearwater

Howard opened the Battle of the Clearwater on that afternoon of July 11 by firing a howitzer at the village from too great a distance. Its shells burst harmlessly in the air overhead. Soon he moved his two howitzers and two Gatling guns to a nearer bluff. Nez Perce warriors led by Rainbow and Ollokot defended the village by fighting from a ravine leading up to the soldiers' position, and from atop another bluff between the ravine and the village. Indian sharpshooters soon picked off the artillery crew, and other warriors led by Toohoolhoolzote nearly surrounded one of the howitzers and one of the Gatling guns. The soldiers made two charges, fighting in the open for half an hour, to push the Nez Perces off the bluff top. Most military casualties of the battle happened during these few minutes.

A few days later, 1st Lieutenant Melville C. Wilkinson described how the Nez Perces fought and concealed themselves:

> They ride up behind little elevations, throw themselves from their ponies, fire, and are off like rockets. Lines of them creep and crawl and twist themselves through the grass until within range, and with pieces as good as ours tell with deadly aim that they are marksmen. They tie grass upon their heads, so that it is hard to tell which bunch of grass does not conceal an Indian with a globe-sighted rifle. They climb trees and shoot from them. (Greene, Nez Perce Summer 1877, p. 89)

During the hot afternoon, Nez Perce sharpshooters kept soldiers from refilling their canteens at a spring near the village. After the shooting stopped around 9:00 P.M., though, the men—including General Howard himself—made several trips to collect sorely needed water. The soldiers went overnight without food and fires.

At nine o'clock the next morning, Captain Marcus P. Miller led a party that captured the spring. Cooks made coffee and bread, and passed them around the lines.

Nez Perce leaders were surprised that Howard did not charge or surround the village and thought it was because he understood how much they wanted him, in particular, dead. White Bird later told Joseph, "If Howard has been as bold as...[Col. John] Gibbon [was, at the later Battle of the Big Hole], we might have been all taken, although we intended to fight to the last" (Laughy, p. 244).

In mid-afternoon on the battle's second day, Looking Glass ordered that the village be packed up and moved. As Joseph said, "It seems...that Looking Glass was a better general than Howard, as he withdrew his camp from the front of the enemy and moved away without the loss of either women, children, horses or lodges" (Laughy, p. 244). As soon as the camp began to move, the Nez Perce warriors left the battle and hurried to join it. When soldiers at last charged from the bluff down the ravine, they could not ford Clearwater Creek and so did not pursue the fleeing rear guard.

The village moved to near Kamiah, pickets (sentries) staying alert all night for a new attack, while people tended the six wounded warriors (three men had died in the battle, and one of the wounded soon died). Yellow Wolf had received a bullet in his left arm near the wrist, which stayed permanently under the skin, and a rock or bullet had grazed his face under the left eye; he stated, "That eye was dimmed for the rest of my life" (McWhorter, *Yellow Wolf*, p. 96).

Howard's command stayed camped on the Clearwater, burying their twelve dead and treating their twenty-seven wounded, including two men who later died. Anything the Nez Perces had left behind, they burned. Despite Joseph's statement of no Indian losses, historian Jerome A. Greene states that the move was ordered too quickly for the women to pack properly, and some food caches, clothing, and even lodges had been left behind.

On July 13, the army followed the Nez Perce trail nine miles to Kamiah, where they could see the village and its livestock herd on a ridge above the Indian agency. Howard had the artillery fired at the Indians and sent Captain Perry's cavalry to charge their position. When the Nez Perces laid down solid fire, many soldiers jumped from their mounts to hide in a grain field.

Howard again let the village move on while his men rested and used the Middle Fork of the Clearwater for their first baths and clothes-washing in weeks. Raiding cattle and horses en route, the Nez Perces went to Weippe Prairie and started over their "road to the buffalo," the Lolo Trail through the Bitterroot Mountains to Montana.

General Howard sent cavalry troops ahead with six treaty Nez Perce scouts to verify that the Indians indeed were using that trail. If they were not, he would go a more roundabout way that was easier riding. East of Weippe Prairie, these men were fired on by the Nez Perce rear guard, and one scout was killed and two wounded.

The Nez Perce truly were leaving Idaho by following the rugged mountain path called the *Nee-Me-Poo* (the Nez Perce) Trail or, today, the Lolo Trail. They also thought they were leaving the war behind.

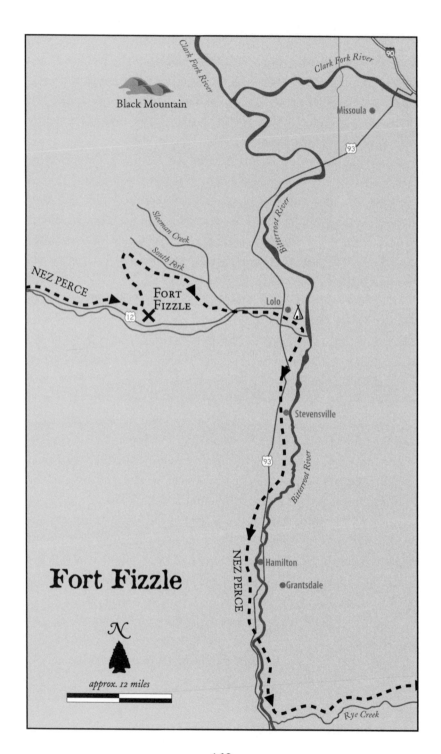

Black Mountain

Clark Fork River

Clark Fork River

Missoula

Sleeman Creek

South Fork

NEZ PERCE

FORT FIZZLE

Lolo

Bitterroot River

Stevensville

NEZ PERCE

Bitterroot River

Hamilton

Grantsdale

Fort Fizzle

N

approx. 12 miles

Rye Creek

# FORT FIZZLE
## — 1877 —

Chief Joseph later recalled that the nontreaty Nez Perce village took nine days to travel from Clearwater, Idaho Territory, to Lolo, Montana Territory. Their path was the established trail that the Nez Perces and the Shoshones regularly used to go from Idaho west of the Bitterroot Mountains—up ridges and down steep ravines again and again—into Montana or Wyoming, where they periodically hunted bison.

General Oliver O. Howard and his command followed, but they were well behind. They did not leave Kamiah until July 30—two weeks after the Nez Perces did. During this summer, the Nez Perces would jokingly change Howard's name from Cut Arm to "Day Behind" because he continued to follow them, but never very closely.

As the Nez Perces moved into Montana Territory, the leaders of the five independent bands continued to meet and discuss what to do when they arrived on the east side of this Rocky Mountains range. Chief Joseph and his younger brother Ollokot thought they should circle back to the part of Idaho south of where they had lived, the Salmon River and Snake River country. White Bird presented the case for heading north through Flathead Indian lands to Canada, to join Sitting Bull's people who had gone there after defeating the army at the Battle of the Little Bighorn. Chief Looking Glass and others thought the people should continue farther east in Montana, to the reservation of their longtime friends and allies, the Crows. Finally, the Looking Glass group carried the day. But, in the Nez Perce way, the chiefs suggested what their people should do, and then each band and each individual decided whether or not to follow the advice.

As the Nez Perces made the difficult passage up the steep forested slopes and along the ridges of the Lolo Trail, they apparently believed that by leaving Idaho Territory, they had ended the fighting. They did not realize that General Howard would call upon other soldiers in the District of Montana to block passage of the fleeing bands and prevent their spilling into the Missoula or Bitterroot valleys. Nor did they understand that the army still had the duty to send them to a reservation.

## Nez Perces Reach Montana

The eastern end of the Lolo Trail was at today's town of Lolo, where the same-named creek flows into the Bitterroot River. Ranch families in the Bitterroot Valley had been following news of the Idaho events, and now they rushed to arrange defenses. Some patched up the old trading post of Fort Owen at Stevensville, and Corvallis residents built a sod stockade divided into rooms by wagon boxes. Another citizen-built defensive position was thrown up near present-day Grantsdale. Ranchers took their wives and children to stay in the valley's string of small settlements, stocked up on ammunition, and braced to defend their homes.

What Howard and the army now hoped to do was bottle up the Nez Perce village before it moved into the Bitterroot Valley. As Howard's command labored up and down on the Lolo Trail, other forces were being gathered and sent to western Montana to help stop the Indians and make them surrender. Howard, however, did not want citizen militias fighting the Indians. He would have been appalled had he heard about territorial governor Benjamin F. Potts's arrival in Missoula on July 26. Potts was calling for volunteers to go with him "to the front."

At that front, the army presence was under the command of Captain Charles C. Rawn, who had arrived at Missoula only a month before to build a military post near town and some sixteen miles north of Lolo Creek. The U.S. Army had authorized the post in 1876, and began construction on June 25, 1877, one year to the day after the Battle of the Little Bighorn. Captain Rawn took his Company I and Captain William Logan's Company A of the Seventh Infantry from Fort Shaw to garrison the post, then located four miles southwest of Missoula. (The following November, their home base would be named Fort Missoula. It was part of Colonel John Gibbon's District of Western

Montana, headquartered at Fort Shaw, and within General Alfred Terry's Department of Dakota.)

Rawn's immediate job in the Nez Perce War was to try to hold the Indians at the mouth of Lolo Creek until Howard caught up, keep the peace and, if at all possible, convince the Indians to surrender. He informed his commanders that he had heard that White Bird would "go through [the Bitterroot Valley] peaceably, if he can, but will go through. This news is entirely reliable" (Greene, *Nez Perce Summer 1877*, p. 109). The captain also obtained a promise from Flathead Indian residents that they would not aid the Nez Perces, their old allies.

On July 25, Rawn took three officers, thirty-four soldiers and fifty civilian volunteers six miles up the Lolo Trail and began to entrench in what he thought the "most defensible and least-easily flanked part" of the canyon. As the men began building their defenses, advance Nez Perce scouts fired on them, just once so they knew now that the Indians were aware of their presence.

The infantrymen and a growing number of citizen volunteers dug an angular rifle trench, plus a few rifle pits, and felled trees to arrange log breastworks in front of them, along a bench that overlooked the creek from the north. Although they were indeed at a narrow spot of the trail, the log-and-earth barricades were open to sharpshooter fire from high peaks on both sides of the canyon. Volunteer Wilson B. Harlan recalled that "it was the belief of most of us, that in case of a fight, especially before our reinforcements arrived, it would have been another Custer massacre" (Greene, *Nez Perce Summer 1877*, p. 110).

The next day, July 26, while his infantry men and the volunteers prepared, and Governor Potts postured in Missoula, Captain Rawn started up the Lolo Trail to meet with the Nez Perce leaders. Looking Glass and White Bird received him cordially and heard what he wanted, that they surrender their weapons, ammunition, and horses. Rawn said he could not guarantee that no one would be hanged for the Idaho raids, because a court would have to decide. The men agreed to meet again the following day after the chiefs counciled with others.

That night, Looking Glass recalled to the council how he had tried to surrender in Idaho, but instead was attacked. He addressed their fear that all the leaders might be hanged at once, and laughingly referred to the breastworks as "The Soldiers' Corral."

> *The soldiers lie so that I have no more confidence in them. They have had their way for a long time; now we must have ours.... If the officer wishes to build corrals for the Nez Perces he may, but they will not hold us back. We are not horses. The country is large. I think we are as smart as he is and know the roads [that is, trails] and mountains as well. (McDonald, p. 249)*

When Captain Rawn returned to the Nez Perces on July 27, he took one hundred armed men, including Governor Potts, and the Nez Perces sensed an attack. But, at Looking Glass's request, Rawn met alone with the chief and an interpreter between the village and the soldiers. Looking Glass offered to surrender his people's ammunition to show that they intended to go peacefully through the Bitterroot Valley, but Rawn declined. His superiors required that he have their guns, too. Looking Glass pointed out how "foolish" it was to think of the Nez Perces going "to buffalo country and not carrying a single gun."

Again, Looking Glass asked for time to meet with other leaders in the Nez Perce way. This time, Rawn said, they would have to send a messenger to his armed camp—"The Corral"—under a truce flag with their reply. After the meeting, Governor Potts returned to Missoula, ending his participation in the Nez Perce War. When the Nez Perce leaders met, they agreed to Looking Glass's plan for the next day. Near "The Corral," the women were to divert up mountain slopes north of the Lolo Trail and the creek and then go down the drainage of Sleeman Creek's south fork, east of the soldiers' barrier. The warriors would cover them from the northern ridges if the soldiers discovered the deceptive move and attacked the exposed women.

At the barricades, most of the volunteers—having heard of the Indians' intention not to fight—simply packed up and went home. The soldiers and a few remaining volunteers spent a sleepless night, made more uncomfortable by light rain, worrying about what would happen in the morning. They well knew how many times so far this year the Nez Perces had bested the U.S. Army.

## An Easy Bypass

About 9:00 A.M. on July 28, pickets reported that the Nez Perces were packed and moving. Instead of advancing on the Lolo Trail to the breastworks, they began climbing the steep terrain, a quarter mile west of Rawn's entrenchment. The warrior Yellow Wolf recalled,

> *We found a different way to go by those soldiers. While a few warriors climbed among rocks and fired down on the soldier fort, the rest of the Indians with our horse herds struck to the left of [the] main trail. I could see the soldiers from the mountainside where we traveled. It was no trouble, not dangerous, to pass those soldiers. (McWhorter, Yellow Wolf, p. 107)*

One of Rawn's officers prepared for an attack from the rear, but the Nez Perces filed down the dry creek bed and into the Bitterroot Valley, hugging for a while the west bank of the Bitterroot River.

Before dark, the Indians were encamped in the Bitterroot Valley, and Captain Rawn had abandoned the breastworks and taken his soldiers back to the post at Missoula. Volunteers even stopped to visit the Nez Perce camp, where Looking Glass received them in a friendly manner.

Territorial newspapers were furious with Rawn's not attacking—despite his not having orders to do so—and with what they saw as a failure of nerve. One wit dubbed the entrenchment "Fort Fizzle," the name that stuck.

As the Nez Perces, who considered the war ended, calmly started south up the Bitterroot River, false rumors of a bloody battle at Lolo Creek preceded them. Shortly, though, as the volunteers reached their homes and word spread of their experience, settlers learned the truth. Instead of attacking the 250 people sheltered at Fort Owen, the Nez Perces had camped three miles away—and went into nearby Stevensville the next day to shop at general stores. Flour was in great demand, along with ammunition and, for some men, whiskey. Looking Glass and other warriors policed the street while their people stocked up on supplies on July 29 and 30, paying some $1,200 in cash and precious metals to Stevensville's few merchants. Some stores raised their prices, but one merchant simply locked his doors.

Since the Salish refused to aid them, Nez Perce leaders now debated whether their Crow allies would welcome them or turn them away. Looking Glass still believed the Crows could not be turned against the Nez Perce people. He sweetened his argument by saying that he knew the intervening country well. If he stayed in charge, he would lead them around the scattered mining camps, lessening the chance of friction with whites.

To General Oliver O. Howard, though, the war was not over. On July 30, while the Nez Perces completed their shopping, his troops mounted up and pulled out of Kamiah onto the Lolo Trail. The following day, Governor Potts again requested volunteers to support the army against the Nez Perces. Responses came at once from larger towns and the little mining camps that Looking Glass intended to avoid. Just as promptly, the War Department turned down Potts's offer; it had plenty of trained soldiers headed toward Montana.

In fact, Colonel John Gibbon was approaching with more than one hundred troops collected from various Montana posts. By the time he started south along the Bitterroot River on August 4, he had added Captain Rawn and three more companies to his command. Moving in contracted civilian wagons more quickly than the Nez Perces' twelve to fifteen miles a day, he was soon gaining on them. With Gibbon, as he had been the previous year in the Great Sioux War, was Lieutenant James H. Bradley, again serving as chief of scouts.

As August began, the Nez Perces left the Bitterroot Valley at Rye Creek and headed for Ross's Hole. From that point they moved southeast into the Beaverhead Mountain range and, fatefully, east to the wide high-mountain valley that mountain men had named the Big Hole. While they marched, some young Nez Perce men raided the Myron Lockwood ranch—taking two hundred pounds of flour and thirty or so of coffee. Looking Glass made them leave horses as payment for supplies taken. Lockwood, who would be wounded in the Big Hole Battle, was not able to return home for some weeks. When he did, he wrote to the local paper that the payment horses were "worn-out worthless cayuses...scarcely able to walk..." and that the paper should not have praised the Nez Perces for leaving them (Haines, p. 28). But there had been no fighting. After all, the chiefs believed they had made it clear to Captain Rawn at Lolo Creek that the war was ended.

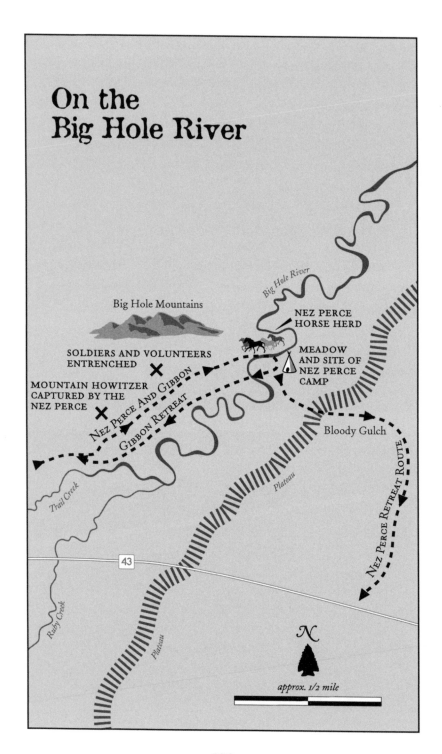

On the
Big Hole River

Big Hole Mountains

Big Hole River

NEZ PERCE
HORSE HERD

SOLDIERS AND VOLUNTEERS
ENTRENCHED

MEADOW
AND SITE OF
NEZ PERCE
CAMP

MOUNTAIN HOWITZER
CAPTURED BY THE
NEZ PERCE

NEZ PERCE AND GIBBON

GIBBON RETREAT

Bloody Gulch

Trail Creek

Plateau

NEZ PERCE RETREAT ROUTE

43

Ruby Creek

Plateau

N

approx. 1/2 mile

# BIG HOLE BATTLE
# — 1877 —

On the night of August 8, 1877, the Nez Perces held a dance at their camp on the North Fork of the Big Hole River, which at that spot meandered from southwest to northeast. The warrior Yellow Wolf recalled:

> *That night the warriors paraded about camp, singing, all making a good time. It was first since war started. Everybody with a good feeling. Going to the buffalo country! No more fighting after Lolo Pass. War was quit. All Montana citizens our friends. (McWhorter, Yellow Wolf, p. 110)*

The chiefs had stopped sending out scouts and keeping a watch for following soldiers because, after all, the war was over. White Bird argued that they were relaxing too much, traveling too slowly, but Looking Glass insisted there was no danger. The latter even ignored Lone Bird, a medicine man who had dreamed that Death was approaching, when he urged the chiefs to move through the open Big Hole valley quickly. Some people said they had seen figures moving in the hills behind them, but Looking Glass said the soldiers were too few to attack and probably were just keeping track of the Nez Perces.

Finally, the warrior Five Wounds said, "All right, Looking Glass, you are one of the chiefs! I have no wife, no children to be placed fronting the danger that I feel coming to us. Whatever the gains, whatever the loss, it is yours" (Nez Perce National Historic Trail website). And so the camp on the stream's east side was at rest at 4:00 A.M. on August 9.

Then chaos erupted. Soldiers attacked from across the creek, shooting low into the lodges and killing men, women, and children in their robes as they charged. Second Lieutenant Charles E. S. Woodruff, one of the soldiers, remembered:

**177**

*The yells of the soldiers, the wild war-whoops of the Indians, the screams of the terrified women and children, the rattle of rifle shots, shouts of command, the cursing of the maddened soldiers already setting fire to the nearest teepees, contributed to the horrors of the battle, which was made more terrible by the presence of mothers and babies in the blue rifle smoke that made the dawn more dim. (Wood, p. 139)*

Firing back, some Nez Perces fled into the creek banks' brush. White Bird and Looking Glass soon rallied the warriors, shouting, "These soldiers cannot fight harder than the ones we defeated on Salmon River and in White Bird Canyon. Fight! Shoot them down."

By then, soldiers were in the village, trying to set fire to the lodges—which were too wet with dew to burn—and lassoing them to pull them down. Nez Perce people of all ages fought hand to hand among their lodges. Captain William Logan, who had just shot a Nez Perce man, was ordering his own troops not to fire on noncombatants when that man's sister plucked up his gun and killed Logan. Boys and women fought the soldiers armed only with knives—and were smashed with rifle butts.

*Yellow Wolf described the close fighting: "We could hit each other with our guns. It was for the lives of women and children we were fighting. If whipped, better to die than go in bondage with freedom gone." (McWhorter, Yellow Wolf, p. 120)*

During this part of the fight, he

*made an advance against some soldiers. Got close enough to take good aimed shots. Three of those same enemies went down. I only know I shot fast and saw each time a soldier fall. I rushed in. Took guns and cartridge belts from those three soldiers. That is the custom of war. Those guns afterwards were used by other Indians. (McWhorter, Yellow Wolf, p. 120)*

People on both sides got powder burns because the firing was so close. Some Nez Perces tried to escape by jumping into the North Fork covered by blankets, but the soldiers quickly recognized the ruse and fired on any blanket in the water.

Within twenty minutes, Colonel John Gibbon's force held the camp. But the Nez Perces would not give up so easily.

## Gibbon on the Trail

After the Nez Perces had left the Bitterroot Valley, Gibbon's command followed their trail. He led six companies of the Seventh Infantry, a mounted detachment of eight cavalrymen from the Second Cavalry, companies posted at Fort Ellis near Bozeman, plus thirty-four civilian volunteers from the Bitterroot Valley. In addition to the wagons transporting the infantrymen, a team pulled a mountain howitzer.

On August 7, two days before the Big Hole attack, Gibbon had accepted Lieutenant James Bradley's suggestion that he move ahead with sixty mounted men. They would make a night march, reach the Nez Perce camp, and stampede the horse herd. The camp was farther ahead than believed, though, and Bradley's party did not reach it until daylight. Sending a messenger back to Gibbon, he and his men hid on August 8.

Gibbon pushed his men forward—often over boggy ground and mazes of downed lodgepole pine—all day. He wanted to reach Bradley before the Nez Perces discovered them. Gibbon's men caught up with Bradley's group at sunset, parked the wagons and rested until 11:00 P.M. in a fireless camp with only hardtack to eat and water to drink. The men were not even allowed to light their pipes. (Hot coffee and warm pipes, historian Kermit Edmonds has observed, were a frontier soldier's basic comforts, and these men had neither.)

When they moved out toward the Nez Perce camp, each man carried his rifle with ninety rounds of ammunition in his recently-received canvas-and-leather "prairie" cartridge belt. The men of Companies A and I brought their experimental trowel-bayonets in scabbards, but all left without items that would be noisy and heavy, including, unfortunately, many individuals' canteens. The mountain howitzer and its fixed ammunition in the limber's two chests, plus two 1,000-round boxes of rifle ammunition, was to be sent forward at dawn. A pack mule would carry it from the hidden wagon park, five miles west of the Nez Perce camp.

At about 2:00 A.M., they were close enough to the camp to hear the occasional dog barking or baby crying, and they stopped and lay in wait for two hours. For the charge, Gibbon assigned Lieutenant Bradley and the volunteers to the left flank, at the camp's north end. To his south, Captain James M. J. Sanno would lead Company K toward the camp's center, and the right flank was assigned to Company D under Captain Richard Comba. While these companies charged across the low, marshy ground and crossed the North Fork, Companies F, G, and I would wait in reserve.

Nearly as soon as the charge began, Bradley was killed. His volunteers, being untrained, faltered and then worked their way to the right to join Sanno's men. This gave the northern part of the village a little more time to react and organize their defense.

One of the early Nez Perce casualties was Red Moccasin Top, whose Idaho raids with Shore Crossing and Swan Necklace had started this war, in Nez Perce eyes. Just the day before, Shore Crossing had told of dreaming that his own death was coming soon. The moment he heard of his friend's death, according to Chief Joseph, he charged straight at the soldiers and was killed. To Joseph, the pair thus "expiate[d] their offense, and…died as brave as the bravest" (McDonald, p. 261).

Animal Entering a Hole (Elaskolatat) and Helping Another (Penahwenonmi), the wife of Wounded Head, told the story differently. They said Shore Crossing was with his pregnant wife, firing while lying on the ground. After Shore Crossing rose up and killed one soldier, another shot him, and Short Crossing fell on his back, dead. His wife then grabbed his gun and killed the second soldier, bringing a rain of bullets at herself. She was shot and died, falling across her husband's body as if protecting him (McWhorter, *Yellow Wolf*, pp. 135, 136).

## Skilled Sharpshooters

After the surprise charge got the soldiers into the village, Nez Perce warriors took to higher ground and began firing down. In his official report, Gibbon stated: "At almost every crack of a rifle from the distant hills, some member of the command was sure to fall." After two hours of trying to destroy the village while his men were being picked off, Gibbon ordered Rawn to form a skirmish line to cover a retreat. Taking what wounded they could, soldiers began moving back to the west, out of the camp. Nez Perces pushed in after them and some combat again was hand to hand.

The howitzer arrived, set up in battery 1,000 yards to the southwest on a mountain slope, and began firing on the village just as Gibbon's men retreated to the creek's west side and entrenched on an elevated alluvial fan of ground, above the creek. Its crew got off only two rounds before Nez Perce warriors ascended the slopes and surrounded them, killing one corporal and wounding two other soldiers. Peopeo Tholekt removed the howitzer barrel from its carriage and rolled the wheels down the bank onto marshy ground. Other Nez Perces dismantled the howitzer's ammunition, captured the rifle ammunition boxes, and threw the gunners' accessories into the sagebrush and trees.

Pinned down in their trenches by sharpshooter fire, Gibbon's men had to get through the day without water. The Nez Perces could have outlasted the soldiers, but among Gibbon's wounded left behind in the Nez Perce camp was a volunteer who told them that Howard's troops were not far behind. He added that a citizen militia was also coming from Virginia City.

Sharpshooters continued to fire throughout the night at anyone who moved in the soldiers' entrenchment. Some soldiers succeeded in getting water, but at least one was killed while doing so. But on the morning of August 10, in sight of the soldiers, the village packed up and moved away while a rear guard of the best warriors kept the soldiers pinned down. Because of his casualties, Gibbon did not even consider following the Nez Perces.

Both sides suffered severe losses. Among the seventy-eight dead the Nez Perces counted, a majority of forty-eight were women and children, many killed in their beds. Fewer warriors had been killed, thirty of them—but they included some of the best ones, such as Five Wounds and Rainbow. Gibbon's command had twenty-nine men killed and forty wounded, two of them mortally.

Now, Looking Glass, who had been so wrong in his thinking about the Nez Perces' safety in the Big Hole valley, was no longer the main leader. That position was given to Lean Elk, known to whites as Poker

Joe. His six lodges had been spending the summer in the Bitterroot Valley and had joined the Nez Perces at Stevensville.

## Into Idaho Territory

After the assault, the Nez Perces traveled south past the fading mining town of Bannack, entering Idaho Territory on August 13 through Bannock Pass, south of Dillon and west of today's Interstate 15. Two days later, on Birch Creek, warriors attacked a train of freight wagons, killing seven men, and on August 16 destroyed the telegraph line at Dubois. White inhabitants gathered and barricaded themselves in small settlements as the Nez Perces continued southeast to Camas Meadows (not to be confused with Camas Prairie) in Idaho, only about seventy miles south of Virginia City, in Montana Territory.

General Howard's troops followed on the trail, passing Bannack on August 15 to the cheers of its residents. Howard's command was 260 men strong, including Bannock Indian scouts from Idaho (led by civilian Stanton G. Fisher) and local volunteers who transported a mountain howitzer from the Montana territorial arsenal in Virginia City. After the scouts located the Nez Perces camped on Camas Meadows, the soldiers made camp on August 19 at the meadow's edge, feasting on fresh trout from what is now called Spring Creek. At 3:30 in the morning, Nez Perce warriors stampeded the volunteers' horses and mules and escaped.

At dawn, Howard sent three companies from the 1st and 2nd Cavalry after them. One company, under Captain Randall Norwood, was cut off while retreating from the Nez Perces. He found depressed ground in a lava flow, hastily threw up rifle pits using lava rocks and aspen trunks, and awaited Howard and the main command. When Howard arrived at about 9:30 A.M., three soldiers were dead and four other soldiers and civilians wounded. He did not pursue the Nez Perces, but treated the wounded and the next day accompanied them to Virginia City. Howard soon sent his command east to Henrys Lake, in Idaho Territory, for four days of rest.

From Virginia City, Howard telegraphed news of the latest defeat to his commander, General McDowell, in San Francisco, who in turned notified General of the Army William T. Sherman. The latter happened to be at Fort Shaw in Montana Territory; he had just toured the two new Yellowstone River forts built after the Great Sioux War and taken a side trip through Yellowstone National Park. Messages sped back and forth in a three-way telegraph correspondence on August 24. When Howard pleaded that his men and their horses were exhausted—having been on the move since starting across the rugged Lolo Trail nearly four weeks before—Sherman snapped: "If you are tired, give the command to some young energetic officer." Howard, sensitive to being in his late forties, replied: "It was the command, including the most energetic young officers, that were worn out and weary by a most extraordinary march" (Greene, *Nez Perce Summer 1877*, p. 164).

By August 31, Sherman had moved to Deer Lodge, closer to the action, and decided to replace Howard in the campaign. To save face for Howard, he would explain that Howard had pursued the Nez Perces past the limits of his military Department of the Columbia. The public could think that the general was merely being called back from Montana to his assigned jurisdiction. Sherman's attitude toward the Nez Perces had become exactly what the Indian leaders feared. He wired Howard that the Indians should be captured or forced to surrender "without terms." To set an example, "[t]heir horses, arms and property should be taken away. Many of their leaders executed...for their murders...[and the rest] sent to some other country," not their homeland (Greene, *Nez Perce Summer 1877*, p. 168).

While Howard had been making his way to Virginia City, the Nez Perces traveled east to the West Fork of the Madison River and followed it into "Wonderland," the five-year-old Yellowstone National Park. They still were heading to Crow country.

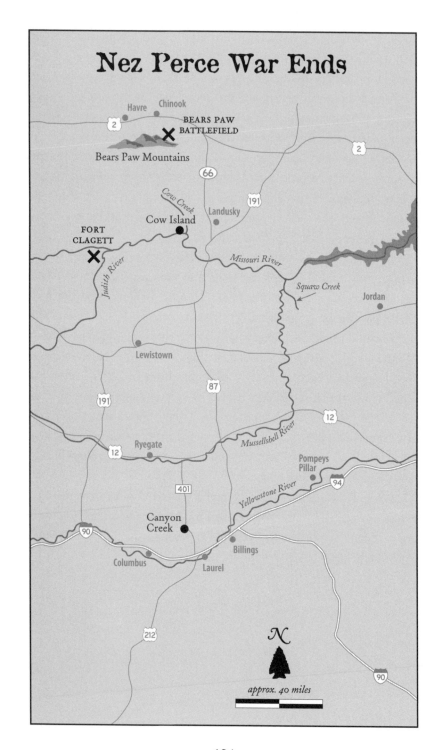

# Nez Perce War Ends

# CANYON CREEK
# AND COW ISLAND
# — 1877 —

In August 1877, while the Nez Perces were out of Montana Territory, Colonel Nelson A. Miles began preparing for their return, expecting they would enter near the Yellowstone River country where he was assigned. When he and his troops joined the Nez Perce campaign, the ambitious colonel no doubt hoped he would be as successful as he had been when he entered the Great Sioux War late in its course.

Partly in reward for his victories over the Sioux the previous spring, Miles was named commander of the army's District of the Yellowstone when it was created on September 4, 1877. From his headquarters at Tongue River Cantonment (soon to be named Fort Keogh), just west of Miles City, he commanded Fort Custer, on the Bighorn River at the Little Bighorn's mouth, by today's Hardin; Fort Peck; and any troops from Fort Buford, Dakota Territory, that might be sent into the field in his domain.

Miles hoped to be promoted to general, but that would not come for years. But in February 1877 he already believed that "it has fallen to my lot to successfully engage larger bodies of Indians than any other officer, and to have gained more extensive knowledge of this remote frontier than any living man" (Greene, *Nez Perce Summer 1877*, p. 247).

A month before the new district was created, in early August 1877, Miles had sent Lieutenant Gustavus Doane and Company E of the Seventh Cavalry, with sixty Crow scouts, out from Tongue River Cantonment. Doane was to proceed to central Montana's Musselshell River country to patrol for Nez Perces. Miles's orders were for Doane to "capture or destroy" the Indians and try to convince the Crows not to welcome their old allies. The Musselshell roughly parallels the Yellowstone

River, forty or so miles north of it, to near Melstone, where it turns north. If the Nez Perces entered that area, they were surely either heading to Canada to join Sitting Bull's Sioux or, worse yet in army leaders' opinions were expecting those Sioux to unite with them in Montana.

In fact, Sitting Bull and his chiefs had discussed doing just that. But Major James M. Walsh, superintendent of the North-West Mounted Police, informed them that if the Sioux warriors returned to the United States, their sanctuary in Canada would end. He would drive their women and children across the border, too. Even while some Nez Perces continued to hope that the Sioux would come to their aid, the Sioux chiefs had already decided against doing so.

Doane, who had joined the regular army after serving in a Civil War volunteer unit, was well qualified for this scouting assignment. He had fought in the Great Sioux War, and two years before had led a formal survey of central Montana's Judith Basin. Before Yellowstone National Park was created, he had led the Washburn-Doane exploration survey of the Yellowstone area.

In mid-August, Miles additionally sent Colonel Samuel D. Sturgis from Tongue River Cantonment to the Judith Basin prairie between the Little Belt and Big Snowy Mountains, north of the Musselshell. During the next four weeks, Sturgis and his six companies of the Seventh Cavalry ranged from the Musselshell River as far south as the Stinking Water in northern Wyoming, watching for the Nez Perces' arrival.

Sturgis had been Colonel George A. Custer's commander at Fort Abraham Lincoln. After the Battle of the Little Bighorn, in which his son 2nd Lieutenant James G. Sturgis was killed, Colonel Sturgis had commanded the Seventh Cavalry's surviving companies in Colonel Miles's spring 1877 campaign against the Sioux and the Northern Cheyennes.

Late in August, before the District of the Yellowstone was created and put under Miles's command, District of Montana commander Colonel John Gibbon ordered Doane's battalion south and into the national park.

## Yellowstone National Park

Yellowstone, the world's first national park, was a remote wilderness that few tourists visited in 1877. Those who did arrived by wagon to the

3,564-square-mile refuge at Wyoming's northwestern corner. They did their exploring by bumping along the few dirt tracks in wagons or walking its few trails.

Traveling down a tributary of the Madison River, about eight hundred Nez Perces entered the park from a small strip of today's Montana that extends between Idaho and Wyoming. Park status meant nothing to them that August 22; this was merely land on their new path to buffalo country, which they needed to use because of General Oliver O. Howard's troops.

*Samuel D. Sturgis. No date, photograph by D. F. Barry.* COURTESY MONTANA HISTORICAL SOCIETY.

Colonel Charles C. Gilbert had just left Fort Ellis with a company of the Second Cavalry. He was General of the Army William T. Sherman's choice to replace Howard in the campaign. Rather than being "some young energetic officer," as Sherman had implied he wanted, Gilbert was eight years older than Howard. During the Civil War, Gilbert had been shifted to desk duty after an undistinguished battlefield record. But Sherman was convinced that Gilbert knew the Yellowstone River country better than Howard. Before he could take over, however, Gilbert had to locate Howard. He never did, but he took over Doane's command to the latter officer's great frustration, then wore out his own horses and Doane's, and returned to Fort Ellis having accomplished nothing.

The Nez Perces crossed the park in about eight days as they traveled east on the Madison River and south on the Firehole to Lower Geyser Basin, then followed the East Firehole River on their way to the Mud Geysers along the Yellowstone River. Just north of Yellowstone Lake, they turned northwest on Pelican Creek and probably east through Hoodoo Basin to exit the park.

One day into their trek through the park, the Nez Perces came upon prospector and ex-soldier John Shively, who was passing through after leaving the Black Hills. They asked him to guide them across the park (fifty-four miles) to Wyoming's Wind River country on its east side. Shively believed he had better agree, travelling unharmed with the Nez Perces until September 2, when he escaped. Like other Americans, Shively had thought Chief Joseph was the "head chief" and now thought he had been demoted when he saw Joseph handling camp logistics.

On August 24, some Nez Perces came upon tourists in the Lower Geyser Basin. Packing their camp near Fountain Geyser, ready to leave for home in Radersburg, Montana Territory, were husband and wife George F. and Emma Cowan, her sister and brother Ida and Frank Carpenter, and Charles Mann and teamster Henry "Harry" Meyers. Also in the group were three of Frank's friends from Helena: Andrew J. Arnold, William Dingee, and Albert Oldham. A Colorado prospector traveling on his own, William H. Harmon, was camped nearby.

As they were eating breakfast, the tourists were surrounded by a small party of Nez Perce warriors, who took all their belongings, destroyed their two wagons, and swapped some tired horses for their fresh ones. After those warriors left, and Harmon joined the party, an even smaller warrior group returned, claiming their chiefs wanted to see the tourists. Both groups of warriors, according to the Nez Perce warrior Yellow Wolf, were "some of the bad boys" among the Nez Perces. George Cowan, who first had resisted giving the Nez Perces the party's food, now was shot and wounded in the head, and Oldham was shot through the cheeks, although without damage to his teeth or tongue.

*After hiding in the brush, all escaped in different directions in ones and twos—all but Emma, Ida, and Frank. The last three were captured when Lean Elk intervened and prevented further killing. They were held for three days and, Chief Joseph said (according to a later account), "They were treated kindly. The women were not insulted. Can the white soldiers tell me of one time when Indian women were taken prisoners...and then released without being insulted?" (McDonald, p. 293)*

Frank Carpenter later said that one of the chiefs (he assumed it was Joseph) apologized for their capture. The trio was released from the Nez Perce camp on the Yellowstone River north of Yellowstone Lake, and given horses and directions to Mammoth Hot Springs near today's North Entrance.

George Cowan, already wounded in the head, now was shot in the hip by the second group of warriors and left for dead. He survived and gradually made his way to help, moving on foot through the park with his dog until August 29, when he met Howard's scouts. All the survivors of this party were reunited at Fort Ellis, where Mrs. Cowan had been recovering when soldiers told her that her husband was alive.

Still another party of tourists—ten men from Helena, Montana Territory—ran afoul of some Nez Perces, who raided their camp for provisions on August 26. Earlier, these men had seen the main group approaching from a distance and realized it was the people so much in the news lately. On August 25, they were joined by James C. Irwin, who had just been released from the military at Fort Ellis and was still wearing his uniform. The eleven men tried to hide on Otter Creek near the Upper Falls, but Nez Perce warriors located them. One man was killed, another received two wounds, Irwin was captured, and the rest escaped—with one of them being killed some days later. Irwin would escape on September 1.

The main body of Nez Perces continued to move on at a brisk pace set by Lean Elk. Historian Jerome A. Greene believes that, even with their captive guides, they took some wrong turns among the curious geological structures of Hoodoo Basin, which delayed their exiting the park until August 30. On that same day, some of the "bad boy" warriors attacked McCartney's Hotel, a solitary log cabin at Mammoth Hot Springs. Northwest of the present-day town of Gardiner, Montana, at Yellowstone's north entrance, they or other warriors attacked the Henderson ranch on August 31, trying to take horses, and killed one of the Helena men who had escaped them earlier. Lieutenant Doane, just then making his way to the park, saw the smoke and charged in. He sent his men after the warriors, who were heading back into the park, and retrieved some of the ranch's horses.

The day before the Nez Perces left Yellowstone National Park, General Howard, his 260 troops, supply wagons, and mule herd moved into it from the west. He followed the same path as the Indians to the Mud Geysers, then turned north, downstream on the Yellowstone until he reached today's Lamar River. When Howard reached Soda Butte Creek on the Lamar, he followed it back into Montana Territory.

Getting his supply wagons through the rugged park was a struggle. At Mary Mountain on September 1, the wagons had to be dragged up the mountain and let down the far side by rope. It took them two more days to reach the Yellowstone River, where Howard's troops had been camped since the 1st, enjoying baths and washing their clothes in the hot springs while awaiting the wagons.

James Irwin, the veteran from Fort Ellis who had spent a week as a Nez Perce captive, met up with Howard on September 2, the day after his escape. Irwin told the general as much as he could about what the Indians were planning. He said they had sent couriers to the Crows, and told Howard that he could follow a better wagon route down the Yellowstone River instead of sticking to the Nez Perces' trail. Howard took that advice, but in a couple of days decided to give up on the supply wagons entirely. He released them to go to Fort Ellis and had his stores packed on mules. Howard's command finally left Yellowstone National Park via Soda Butte Creek near Cooke City, Montana.

## Wyoming and Montana on Alert

General Sherman, meanwhile, still thought the Nez Perces might continue east from Yellowstone National Park across Wyoming. He ordered seven cavalry troops from General George Crook's command, led by Colonel Wesley Merritt, into the Wind River country. They never made contact with the Indians, and returned to Camp Brown, Wyoming Territory, late in September.

Colonel Sturgis abandoned his east-of-the-park scouting and turned north, picking up Howard's trail. He joined his command with Howard's on September 8, and they followed the Clarks Fork of the Yellowstone downstream toward its mouth on the Yellowstone River. The two decided that Sturgis would take some of Howard's troops ahead on a forced march to catch up with the Nez Perces, and on September 12 those men set out at 5:00 A.M. Howard sent an alert to Colonel Miles at Tongue River Cantonment to watch for and stop any Nez Perces coming north toward him.

When Miles received the message five days later, he prepared instantly, leaving Tongue River Cantonment the next day. Picking up other troops in the field, his command shortly included 520 men: soldiers in three companies of the Second Cavalry, three of the Seventh, and six companies of the Fifth Infantry, plus scouts (including Northern Cheyennes and Sioux), and civilian packers and teamsters. They traveled toward the mouth of the Musselshell River on the Missouri, moving rapidly at thirty or so miles per day.

Sturgis and his cavalry marched down the Clarks Fork for eighteen hours in cold, pouring rain. When they finally made camp and built bonfires to warm and dry themselves eight miles from the Yellowstone, they had ridden an estimated sixty miles.

The Nez Perces traveled along the north side of the Yellowstone that day, unaware of Sturgis's rapid approach. To avoid the new settlement of Coulson right on the Yellowstone (since absorbed by present-day Billings' west side), the people turned at Canyon Creek, which flows from the northwest into the Yellowstone. Moving a little way upstream on September 12, 1877, the Nez Perces camped on the flat, grassy creek bottom.

## Canyon Creek

The next day, some of the Nez Perce warriors were attracted to the brand-new stagecoach station on Canyon Creek, a half-mile north of the Yellowstone River. Just as a stage pulled in, they raided the station, burning its buildings and the stored hay. The passengers jumped from the coach and hid safely in the brush until the warriors rode on down the Yellowstone. Their next target was the hay and corral on a ranch, and then they came upon a camp of two wolfers—men who made their living by turning in wolf pelts for bounties. The warriors killed both wolfers, but when they met up with the rancher whose land the camp was on, they merely took his horses and did him no harm.

During this extended raid, the main Nez Perce village had packed up and was moving across the open, treeless land up Canyon Creek. Ahead of them, and north of present-day Laurel, was a canyon into which Canyon Creek's North Fork flowed. On its north side, a four-hundred-foot, many-colored rimrock wall rose, across the half-mile-wide canyon from the high point now called Horse Cache Butte. Through the canyon was an easy path up from the Yellowstone River bottom onto higher prairie land. A ridge of land three hundred feet high angled southwest to northeast—the opposite angle from Canyon Creek's flow—its center just under three miles south of the creek and its east end closer.

According to historian Francis Haines, some of the warriors who burned the stage station raced to the main body of Nez Perces, driving the stagecoach and arriving just before Sturgis's command.

Having camped only a few miles behind the Nez Perces the night before, Sturgis's Bannock Indian scouts under Stanton G. Fisher soon reported where the village was, as well as the smoke rising from the distant stage station. Shortly before noon on September 13, from four miles away, the cavalry moved forward at a trot. Sturgis placed Major Lewis Merrill and 150 men in three companies at the lead, and as they closed on the Nez Perces they began firing their rifles. Nez Perce sharpshooters answered from atop the south ridge. Merrill's troops moved directly up the south ridge, dismounted, and began pushing the sharpshooters from its top, which proved to be about a mile wide and three miles long.

As soon as Sturgis reached the ridge top, he considered the lay of the land, noting the canyon mouth three miles beyond the Nez Perces. At once he recognized that his goals were to capture the Nez Perce horses herded by the women and children, and stop the people from entering the canyon's safety. After about thirty minutes of firing from the ridge top, with mounted Nez Perce warriors staying between Merrill's men and the horse herd, the soldiers began moving down the ridge's creek side.

The Nez Perces' advance warriors took positions high atop the canyon opening and began shooting back at the soldiers, covering the women and children so they could escape the battle.

The Crow scouts went after the horse herd, cut three hundred head out of it, and raced them away to their reservation. (A few days later, in the Judith Basin, the Nez Perces would come upon a Crow hunting and meat-preserving camp and kill its members in revenge.) On the Canyon Creek battlefield, Captain Frederick W. Benteen led a sweep toward the herd, trying to capture it. To Yellow Wolf, the horses did not seem to be the target:

> Other soldiers [on] horseback, like cavalry, were off to one side. Away ahead of the walking soldiers. They tried to get the women and children. But some warriors, not many, were too quick. Firing from a bluff, they killed and crippled a few of them, turning them back. (McWhorter, Yellow Wolf, p. 186)

The battle continued as a mobile fight, slowly moving across eight miles as many of the tired cavalry fought on foot, while those on horseback found their mounts slow to move, and the Nez Perces kept pressing toward the canyon. Sharpshooter fire from the Nez Perces atop the canyon walls became too intense, and after moving about five miles toward the canyon, the army once again gave up. To Yellow Wolf, the army had used Crow and Bannock allies because "General Howard's warriors were afraid." He added, "Only when we were moving would they come after us" (McWhorter, *Yellow Wolf*, p. 192). During the entire Battle of Canyon Creek, the Nez Perces had lost only one warrior.

Sturgis's command buried their two dead and treated their eight wounded, including one man whose wounds were mortal. Horses and mules killed in the battle were butchered for fresh meat as Sturgis's main command camped on the battlefield that night. Sturgis's men hit the trail again on September 14, the Nez Perces continuing to outpace them as they moved north and forded the Musselshell River near today's Ryegate.

On September 14, after the main command had moved on but before Lieutenant Charles A. Varnum's escort pulled out with the wounded, General Howard arrived. He had ridden through the night with fifty soldiers after receiving Sturgis's dispatch that he was engaging the Nez Perces. Sending his own command after Sturgis, Howard joined Varnum's group taking the wounded to Pompeys Pillar on the Yellowstone. There they were loaded onto a large, flat-bottomed row-boat/sailboat called a "mackinaw" to go to Tongue River Cantonment.

En route to Pompeys Pillar, Varnum's and Howard's battalion met up with "Calamity Jane," Martha Jane Cannary, who then was living at the Canyon Creek battle site, historian Jerome A. Greene notes. She temporarily traveled with Varnum's command to help care for the wounded men. He said, "Then and for many years after the soldiers expressed their enthusiasm of [sic] her nursing in the highest of terms" (Carroll, p. 21).

With Sturgis's command, 150 Crow warriors, eager to capture more horses, followed and attacked the Nez Perces' rear guard, eventually killing five warriors and taking about four hundred horses. Sturgis endorsed this continuing action because the Crows' horses were fresher than those of his cavalry. Not only were the army horses tired from the constant movement, but they also had developed a hoof disease that further slowed them.

The Nez Perces were surprised and saddened to be attacked by the longtime allies that Chief Looking Glass had been so sure would help them. Yellow Wolf said, "My heart was just like fire.... They were fighting against their best friends!"—the people who had helped the Crows fight a Sioux war party only three years before (McWhorter, *Yellow Wolf*, pp. 187, 194).

By the time Sturgis's command reached the Musselshell on September 15, he had decided they could not continue and would stop there to rest and await resupply from Fort Ellis. Many of the horses could no longer carry riders, and others limped painfully along. Grazing was scarce where bison herds had moved through the open country. The soldiers were completely out of rations, now living on fresh meat from their own dead mounts or bison they hunted, supplemented with ripe berries when available. They camped at the Musselshell near the site of present-day Ryegate for a week until Howard's infantry caught up with them on September 22.

Howard himself, after the side trip to Pompeys Pillar with the Canyon Creek wounded, joined Sturgis two days before the infantry arrived. The combined command now moved westward across the Musselshell and continued after the Nez Perces, entering the Judith Basin on September 25.

Meanwhile, Colonel Miles's large command continued its quick overland movement. It reached the Missouri River at Squaw Creek, a few miles downstream from the mouth of the Musselshell, on September 23. That day a courier from Tongue River Cantonment brought Miles the news of the Canyon Creek battle, and Howard's information that his command had slowed down, hoping that would slow the Nez Perces until Miles reached them.

Today this stretch of the Missouri is part of Fort Peck Lake, but that September 24, Miles had to get his command across only the Musselshell River. Luckily, the steamboat *Fontenelle* was in the area and spent the next day ferrying his men, horses, and wagons west and across. Miles received news of the Cow Island raid the next day. The *Fontenelle* had just pulled out of sight when Miles received the note that one of the Cow Island depot soldiers had sent down the Missouri by mackinaw. Miles was still on the south side of the Missouri and needed to cross it quickly now that he knew where the Nez Perces were headed. Even if it were possible to ford the Missouri at Cow Island, it was impossible just west of the Musselshell. Miles at once had artillery fired to call back the *Fontenelle*, which spent the rest of the day ferrying Miles's command to the Missouri's north side.

## Cow Island

The Nez Perces reached the Missouri River at Cow Island on September 23, crossed to its north side, then traveled a couple of miles farther north on Cow Creek to camp. By autumn, the snowmelt-fed Missouri River was reaching its lowest level for the year. That made the people's crossing at this natural ford easier, but it also meant that steamboats taking freight to Fort Benton—125 river miles up the Missouri from this point—could not get all the way upriver. Before low-water season, Fort Benton was the head of navigation on the Missouri.

On the Missouri's north side, a freight depot had been constructed at Cow Creek. Used for only a short time each year, it consisted of tents inside an earthwork entrenchment built in a willow grove. Steamboats offloaded their freight, which was stored in the tents to await freight wagons or mackinaw boats to take it onward. Four clerks paid by the freight companies kept records and managed the depot. When the Nez Perces passed by, fifty tons of U.S. government and commercial freight sat ready for pickup: dry goods headed for stores, food for the military and the markets, paper, bolts of cloth. Sergeant William Molchert and eleven soldiers were also on hand to protect incoming military supplies.

The quick pace that Lean Elk had set since the people left the Big Hole was wearing hard on them. Their horses, like the cavalry's, also had a hoof disease. By now they figured that the troops of Cut Arm— General Howard—were at least two days behind them. Most people agreed with Looking Glass that they no longer needed to travel so fast, and once again they looked to him as their leader. It was not too far now—roughly eighty miles—to Canada. The Missouri River was the last geographical barrier, and it was past. Besides, they knew from experience how much time the cavalry needed to cross a river.

After the Nez Perces set up their camp, several of the men went back to the freight depot in hopes of buying or being given food from the obviously plentiful stock. They talked with Sergeant Molchert, who gave them a side of bacon and a bag of hardtack, a miserly gift considering how much he seemed to have at hand.

Later in the evening, Nez Perce warriors began to fire on the Cow Island depot, and its denizens sheltered behind their earthwork. The night was pitch black, and Molchert later said that the Indians charged the depot three different times, causing the men inside to fire blindly into the darkness. Two of the civilian clerks were wounded. Nez Perce women and men took food and cooking utensils from the stored freight. Yellow Wolf said, "When everybody had what they wanted, some bad boys set fire to the remaining. It was a big fire!" (McWhorter, *Yellow Wolf*, p. 199).

Molchert thought the only thing that saved his group from being overrun was that the Nez Perces set fire to a large tent filled with bacon, and the fire lit up the area. Now the warriors could not approach without being seen and targeted. But they continued firing into the depot all night and until about 10:00 A.M. the next day, when the chiefs told them to stop. As long as the soldiers and clerks stayed inside their earth-work, shooting at them was just wasting ammunition. The Nez Perces struck camp and moved on.

No Nez Perces were killed in the fight, but this is where Wounded Head got the name by which he is known throughout accounts of the Nez Perce War. A bullet sent a splinter of wood flying, and it cut his head, resulting in a minor wound that bled mightily.

By the time the Nez Perces left the area, the entire depot was burn-ing, and it burned all day on September 24. The Cow Island depot staff were finally rescued after dark that night by a troop of soldiers and civil-ian volunteers. The latter, commanded by Major Guido Ilges, had come down the Missouri from Fort Benton. They had been assigned to protect the trading post of Fort Clagett near the mouth of the Judith River if the Nez Perces turned that way. At Clagett, Ilges learned that the Nez Perces were heading to Cow Island, so he continued downstream. His command also was joined by thirteen more soldiers and thirty-eight civilians, plus a mountain howitzer, which had come down the Missouri in mackinaws.

From Molchert and the depot clerks, Ilges learned of a group of sol-diers and civilians who were now in the Nez Perces' path. A small freight wagon train, driving a herd of beef cattle, was accompanied by a wagon of soldiers and civilians, including four women. Having left the depot on September 22, the group was now making its slow way through Cow Creek Canyon, where the rough trail to Fort Benton crossed Cow Creek thirty-one times. It was slow, muddy going, and the Nez Perces caught up with the train before Ilges's soldiers did.

They camped near it in Cow Creek Canyon, and a few warriors vis-ited the freighters on the evening of September 24. The Nez Perces especially wanted to buy ammunition, according to O. G. Cooper, one of the freighters. He noticed that the natives had all sorts of guns, including military carbines, and he saw army brands on many of their weary, ailing horses.

The next morning, September 25, just as Major Ilges's battalion came into sight, a Nez Perce warrior shot and killed one of Cooper's teamsters. The other wagon train members were able to hide in the shrubs while warriors set the freight wagons afire, took to higher ground, and began firing at the approaching soldiers.

From about noon until 2:00 P.M., Ilges's small command exchanged fire with the Nez Perces, losing one soldier, before Ilges called for a gradual retreat back to Cow Island. After the Nez Perces moved on, Ilges returned to the canyon battle site and buried the soldier and the teamster there before heading back to Fort Benton. Ilges left twenty-five soldiers, with the howitzer, to guard the Cow Island freight depot. He also sent a courier to locate Colonel Miles and give him the news.

The Nez Perces moved on, traveling around the east and northeast sides of the Bears Paw Mountains, where they made their last camp of the Nez Perce War on Snake Creek, on September 29. They were now only forty miles from the Canadian border.

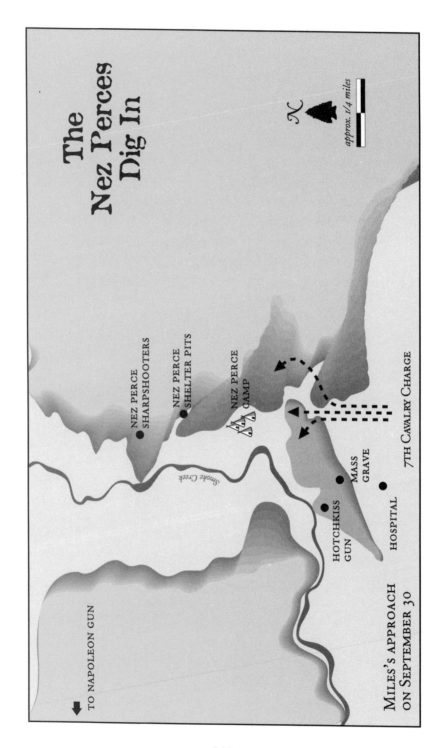

The
Nez Perces
Dig In

approx. 1/4 miles

NEZ PERCE
SHARPSHOOTERS

NEZ PERCE
SHELTER PITS

NEZ PERCE
CAMP

Smoke Creek

7TH CAVALRY CHARGE

MASS
GRAVE

HOTCHKISS
GUN

HOSPITAL

TO NAPOLEON GUN

MILES'S APPROACH
ON SEPTEMBER 30

# BEARS PAW MOUNTAINS
## — 1877 —

The end of the Nez Perce War, and of the nontreaty Nez Perces' eleven-hundred-mile march to escape reservation life, came with a one-day battle and a five-day siege, over the freezing turn of October 1877. The site is just north of the Bears Paw Mountains, locally called "the Bearpaws," and sixteen miles south of where Chinook would be founded after the railroad arrived about a decade later. By the time the Nez Perces surrendered, their numbers were little more than half what they had been when the people tried to move away from the war. Besides those who died before and during this battle, a few hundred would escape to Canada, where a few stayed permanently.

As soon as the *Fontenelle* had ferried Colonel Miles's men to the Missouri River's north side on September 25, they began rushing northwest. They crossed open prairie between the Little Rocky Mountains and, to the west, the Bears Paw Mountains. That was where Cow Creek, which the Nez Perces were following upstream, flowed north toward "the British Possessions." If they had crossed the international border, they would enter what is now Saskatchewan.

On the afternoon of September 27, Miles decided he wanted to move faster than the supply wagons allowed. He left forty soldiers to escort the wagons and the heavy Napoleon gun at the best pace they could. Miles and the rest of the mounted soldiers took the lighter-weight Hotchkiss mountain gun and eight days' rations on pack animals, and pulled out. The Hotchkiss, which fired two-pound shells, was the first light breech-loading mountain artillery piece used by the U.S. Army, and Miles was field-testing it.

Two days later, as Miles's battalion moved northwest through the rolling prairie's dried grass, closing in on the Bears Paw

Mountains, the Nez Perces set up their camp on Snake Creek on the hills' north side. The day had started with a chilly autumn rain, which in the afternoon turned to snowfall that piled up several inches deep. Yellow Wolf was among the Nez Perce warriors watching the back trail, but they were not worried about soldiers drawing close: "We expected none," he said. "We knew General Howard was more than two suns back on our trail. It was nothing hard to keep ahead of him" (McWhorter, *Yellow Wolf*, p. 204).

Chief Looking Glass did not rush the tired people and sore-footed horses forward as Lean Elk had when he was in command. In fact, he said they would get a good night's rest on Snake Creek and not leave too early in the morning. Set on the creek bottom amid a few shrubs and willows, the campsite was surrounded by ravines and low ridges. To its south, a steep bluff rose from the prairie as a gentle hill; the side toward camp, however, was a sheer cutbank. This camp on the east side of Snake Creek was quick to set up and take down because, by now, many lodges had been lost in the battles, and the people had decided to travel without lodgepoles, to speed their progress. There had been no time to tan leather and make new lodge covers, so most people used odd pieces of canvas for shelter.

The nontreaty Nez Perces' numbers had shrunk by at least one hundred from the eight hundred or so who had started out from Idaho—mostly by death under attack and in battle. Of the seven hundred, perhaps only 250 were warriors, according to historian Jerome A. Green, or half the number of Miles's command (Greene, *Yellowstone Command*, p. 266).

## In Snow and Rain

As always, each band had its own grouping in camp, which spread about a quarter-mile long and about two hundred yards wide. Chief Joseph's Wallowa band, combined with the Palouses of Husis Kute, placed their circle at the southern end. From there to the north were Looking Glass's band, White Bird's, and Toohoolhoolzote's.

Beyond the north end of camp, two ridges rose, and between them was a protected coulee. This would become a crucial hiding place for both noncombatants and warriors.

With the Nez Perces unaware of his approach, Miles, also unaware of the Nez Perces' location, camped only about fifteen miles away that snowy night. Although his scouts had been checking on all sides of the battalion, they had not yet found the natives' camp, although they knew it was near. 2nd Lieutenant Marion P. Maus and his party of scouts had come upon some Nez Perce warriors during the day and had taken fourteen of their horses. Late on September 29, Northern Cheyenne scouts reported they had picked up the Nez Perces' trail, off to the left. Miles sent Luther "Yellowstone" Kelly, Lieutenant Maus, and three others back out to search for the main group of Nez Perces. When they had not found it by dark, they camped where they were, away from Miles's battalion.

With no trees and few shrubs on the prairie, all three camps had fires of buffalo chips that night while rain and snow alternated, intensifying the steady wind's chilling effect.

Miles's troops were roused at 2:00 A.M. on September 30 and began their march about two and a half hours later. Their commander went ahead with the scouts—Northern Cheyennes and Sioux painted for battle and riding their special war ponies—to find the Nez Perce camp. Daylight brought a clear, crisp autumn day with the snow melting rapidly. Talking with Little Bighorn survivors Captain Edward S. Godfrey and Captain Myles Moylan just before the order to mount up, Captain Owen Hale said ruefully as he struggled to keep warm, "My God! Have I got to be killed this beautiful morning?" (Greene, *Nez Perce Summer 1877*, p. 264). Hale had served in the Civil War as a volunteer, then joined the Seventh Cavalry afterward.

The cavalry wore their warm but bulky and restrictive winter uniform coats that sported attached short capes over the shoulders. Their colonel, Nelson A. Miles, hid his rank by wearing the uniform trousers of an army private, with a heavy red flannel shirt, a short buckskin jacket, and a slouch hat with a blue ribbon band, its long tails snapping in the breeze.

In their camp, the Nez Perces were packing to move on. Wottolen told Looking Glass about a dream he had had, which indicated they were in great danger of another attack. Just as he had with Lone Bird's dream of approaching death before the Battle of the Big Hole, Looking

Glass dismissed Wottolen's. When scouts rushed in to report bison were stampeding on their back trail—possibly indicating approaching noisy soldiers—Looking Glass told the people there was plenty of time to get going. Let the children finish their breakfasts and eat their fill, he said. As Yellow Wolf put it later, calmly stating the fact to Lucullus McWhorter without complaint: "Because of Chief Looking Glass, we were caught" (McWhorter, *Yellow Wolf*, p. 205).

Not long after 9:00 A.M., Miles had the camp in sight and outlined the assignments for the initial charge. The Northern Cheyenne scouts were to ride in advance on the left, leading Captain George L. Tyler's command into the camp before turning left to cut off the Nez Perce horse herd. Commanding Companies F, G, and H of the Second Cavalry, Tyler was a veteran soldier who had joined the regular army after fighting in a Civil War volunteer unit. On the right, Captain Hale commanded Companies A, D, and his own Company K of the Seventh Cavalry. Captains Moylan and Godfrey of the Seventh had both commanded companies (A and D, respectively, which they now led) that survived the Battle of the Little Bighorn the previous year. Colonel Miles rode near the companies of the Seventh.

Moving in behind those two battalions would come the mounted companies B, F, G, and I of Miles's own Fifth Infantry, followed by Company K of the Fifth on foot with the Hotchkiss gun and wagons.

## "Charge Them!"

At Miles's shout of "Charge them! Damn them!" the battle began, some of the mounted soldiers raising their own battle cries as they galloped at the unsuspecting village. The Nez Perce warriors grabbed horses tethered by their shelters and began firing back, while women and children, many with already-loaded horses, headed for the north end of camp, away from the attack.

Miles stayed back from the charge, constantly riding from side to side to shout orders or send messengers onto the field with the soldiers and sometimes yelling at the Nez Perces to surrender. He changed horses several times during the battle as individual mounts tired because he kept them in constant motion, knowing that he was a prime target for

Nez Perce sharpshooters. Even without any badges of rank, he was obviously the soldiers' war leader.

As the soldiers neared the camp, it became hidden by the bluff just south of it. They rode up the gentle side of the bluff expecting it to curve just as smoothly down to the campsite, and then discovered the nearly vertical cutbank on the far side. A ravine cutting into the east side of the bluff top had forced Captain Hale and Company K to move off to the right during the charge, becoming separated from the main command by three hundred yards. There, they came under intense fire from Nez Perce warriors, and Hale ordered them to dismount and form a skirmish line.

At Hale's left during the charge, Moylan and Godfrey were able to ride straight ahead, but were stopped atop the bluff by its sheer north side. Hale could see that Moylan and Godfrey's blocked commands were under strong fire from twenty or so Nez Perce warriors, including Yellow Wolf, who climbed through ravines up the cutbank. At the top, they popped up directly in front of the troops. In moments, soldier after soldier was shot from his saddle, but the cavalry and mounted infantry were able to hold this bluff throughout the day.

Ollokot, Joseph's brother who had developed as a war leader over the past few months, was killed early on. Chief Toohoolhoolzote fought from a rifle pit near his band's circle at the north end of camp—until a soldier's bullet killed him. Looking Glass, thinking he at last saw a group of Sitting Bull's Sioux coming to help the Nez Perces, stood up in his rifle pit to get a better view. He was killed by a soldier sharpshooter's bullet.

During the attack, the Northern Cheyenne and Sioux scouts veered to the left earlier than they were supposed to and headed directly toward the horse herd, which was three hundred yards west of the village. Captain Tyler, as ordered, had followed their lead, which lessened the charge into the Nez Perce camp by the strength of three companies.

Chief Joseph shouted to the Nez Perces to save the horses, and Yellow Wolf and other warriors ran toward the herd from the north of camp. His view from there of the accidentally divided charge was of "Hundreds of soldiers charging in two wide, circling wings." He said, "They were surrounding our camp" (McWhorter, *Yellow Wolf*, p. 207).

The Cheyennes and Sioux began fighting off the Nez Perces trying to reach their horses, and drove them back into the camp from the southwest while Tyler and his men captured some of the horse herd, even though their movement was slowed by their own horses' infected hooves. Some of the Nez Perce boys who had been watching the herd, and adult men and women—about seventy people in all—managed to escape to the north and begin trekking toward Canada. Tyler sent Lieutenant Edward J. McClernand on what turned into a five-mile running battle with women and children to capture horses they were trying to save from capture. Eventually these soldiers found themselves north of the village—opposite the main command—and temporarily surrounded by Nez Perce warriors on three sides. They managed to pull back, and portions of the Second held positions northwest and northeast of the village.

Yellow Wolf recalled that the Cheyennes' leader said in sign language that his people would shoot only into the air, and all the Nez Perces trying to get their horses were relieved. But after the Cheyenne "rode south about forty steps," he grabbed the bridle of a Nez Perce woman's horse "and with his six-shooter shot and killed the woman. I saw her fall to the ground. We shot at that Cheyenne from where we were" (McWhorter, *Yellow Wolf*, p. 208). But he escaped the Nez Perces' bullets.

Simultaneously, on the opposite side of the Nez Perce camp, Moylan had just reached Hale's isolated company when he was shot in the thigh, and Hale was shot in the spine at the throat and killed. Godfrey's horse was shot and killed, leaving him afoot, but trumpeter Thomas Herwood rode his horse between his captain and the Nez Perces while Sergeant Charles H. Welch fired back at the warriors until Godfrey could escape. 2nd Lieutenant Edwin P. Eckerson, suddenly the only commissioned officer functioning for the Seventh's companies at this point, led the men in retreat, his own horse wounded along the way.

Godfrey found another horse and returned to the front, but soon was shot in his side. Holding his horse's saddle and using its body for cover, he walked back behind the lines to the busy hospital tent.

Many fighters on both sides, including the mounted troops of the Fifth Infantry who had followed the cavalry in the charge, took positions flat on the ground, or even dug rifle pits in the ground. Cavalry troopers who had been holding horses decided that they had to begin fighting and released their charges' reins to take up their guns.

Not long after the initial horseback charge, the men of the Fifth Infantry got the Hotchkiss gun up onto a bluff where it could fire past the protective bluff south into the camp. However, as with the army's howitzer at the Battle of the Big Hole, Nez Perce sharpshooters focused intently on the gun crew, forcing them to stop firing. After nightfall, the gun was moved so it could fire into the coulee where the Nez Perces were entrenched. Near it was a steadily increasing group of blanket-covered dead soldiers removed from the battlefield.

Almost all of the deaths during this engagement happened during the first day's fight. Four Nez Perces, including Lean Elk and Lone Bird, were killed by their own warriors who mistook them for Northern Cheyenne or Sioux scouts. Twenty-two Nez Perces were dead by day's end, as were eighteen soldiers. Forty-six soldiers and two of their Indian scouts were wounded, and the number of Nez Perce wounded is unknown. Yellow Wolf summarized the battle: "I did what I could on the outside with other warriors. But we could not charge close on the soldiers. They were too many for us. The big guns, also, the soldiers had" (McWhorter, *Yellow Wolf*, p. 209).

## Shelter Pits and Tunnels

During the fighting of September 30, Nez Perce women and children moved into the protected coulee north of the camp and began entrenching with any digging tools they had. They dug with knives, the hooks used to harvest camas bulbs, and trowel bayonets taken from dead soldiers at the Big Hole, moving the excavated dirt with cooking pans. Over the course of the afternoon and into the night, they carved forty shelter pits, even connecting some of them with tunnels. They also created two cisterns that filled with water from Snake Creek. The only food they had was dried meat and whatever could be eaten without cooking, because they did not dare build fires. Not that they had much fuel anyway—buffalo chips were the only source of fuel available. Warriors who hid in ravines on the sheltering ridges that protected the coulee dug their own rifle pits.

In the middle of the afternoon, after about six hours of battle, the army commanded positions on the south, west, and north sides of the camp. Miles decided on a two-pronged charge into the camp's south end and sent the mounted Fifth Infantry soldiers, led by Lieutenant Mason Carter, to approach along Snake Creek on the west side. First Lieutenant Henry Romeyn was to move from the east side with the Seventh Cavalry. He was shot and wounded as he stood in his stirrups to wave his hat, starting the charge. The Seventh barely began to move, and then retreated. Carter's troops got all the way into the village but, with no support from the Seventh, retreated at sunset, crawling low to stay hidden from Nez Perce sharpshooters.

As darkness fell, some wounded soldiers lay among their dead comrades in "no man's land" between the lines. They feared being killed and mutilated, unaware that the Nez Perces did not follow this custom. Warriors approached them during the night only to take their guns and ammunition. Firing gradually ceased and a miserable night began, cold wind bringing alternating hail, sleet, and snow. Yellow Wolf returned to his camp. "I did not hurry," he said. "Soldiers guarding, sitting down, two and two. Soldiers all about the camp, so that none could escape from there" (McWhorter, *Yellow Wolf*, p. 210). Nez Perce women wailed their mourning songs, and families buried their dead.

Yellow Wolf would be proved wrong about escaping. Perhaps because the soldiers' vigilance relaxed as the siege lengthened, as many as one hundred Nez Perces did manage to slip away over the next four days. But, as Private William Zimmer later learned, fourteen of the escapees were killed and their horses taken when they came upon a camp of Gros Ventres and Assiniboines, two more tribes that refused to help the Nez Perces (Zimmer, p. 129).

After entering camp, Yellow Wolf drank some water but did not even think about eating. As he moved around and learned who had been killed during the day's fighting, he reacted first with sadness and then with anger. With no blanket for warmth, he joined other warriors in digging rifle pits "all the rest of [the] night," and said that his fury kept him from feeling the cold (McWhorter, *Yellow Wolf*, p. 211).

Miles sent couriers out under cover of darkness to find Colonel Samuel D. Sturgis and his troops, who had been in the Musselshell

River country before Miles engaged the Nez Perces. The couriers reached Sturgis in two days, and he immediately began a quick march, had his troops ferried across the Missouri River by steamboat, and reached the Little Rockies by October 4. Sturgis's couriers, who were carrying his reply to Miles, by chance met General Oliver O. Howard and told him of Miles's situation, causing Howard also to rush toward the Bears Paw Mountains.

At daylight on October 1, soldiers began firing the Hotchkiss gun blindly through the snow-filled air, its shells exploding high over the entrenched Nez Perces. Just as blindly, warriors shot back. In their shelter pits, the women butchered horses killed in battle for fresh meat, cooking it over fires made from their few precious lodgepoles.

With the situation stalemated, Colonel Miles hoped to negotiate a surrender and sent several Northern Cheyenne scouts to the Nez Perces under a flag of truce. With the shooting stopped, both sides quickly gathered their wounded and dead from among the killed horses and ponies lying on the battlefield.

Joseph and five men, including interpreter Tom Hill, a Delaware–Nez Perce mixed blood, walked across to the soldiers' lines and were escorted to Miles's tent. The leaders shook hands and sat down to talk. At the same time, Miles sent 2nd Lieutenant Lovell H. Jerome of the Second Cavalry and some Cheyennes to the Nez Perce camp to report firsthand on its fortifications and warrior strength. Jerome later said he was to note the positions of rifle pits, where best to aim the artillery, and whether the camp could be overrun. His party was received politely. Shortly, a courier from Miles brought Jerome a note.

Joseph told Miles which of the chiefs were already dead and that he wanted to surrender, but many others did not. Miles asked that at least they turn over their guns, but Joseph countered they were needed for hunting. Finding nothing they could agree on, Joseph and his party started back toward their camp. They had walked about twenty-five yards when Miles suddenly called Joseph back—and captured him! The others were allowed to return to the Nez Perce camp with the information.

Miles's note to Jerome had told him to escape from the camp because Miles planned to keep Joseph hostage. But Jerome did not leave immediately and, when word of the capture arrived, he himself was taken prisoner. White Bull wanted to kill Jerome on the spot, but was voted down. Wottolen, the prominent warrior Yellow Bull, and Tom Hill were put in charge of Jerome, who was given two blankets, allowed to keep his pistol, and during the night was even moved from one shelter pit to another for protection from angry Nez Perces. Yellow Bull was allowed to visit Joseph and see how he was. Although Yellow Wolf later recalled that Joseph was trussed up in blankets like a child on a cradleboard, Joseph never said that. His only complaint was that Miles would not give the two men privacy to talk.

The state of siege continued through October 1, with occasional sharpshooting from each side. One more soldier was killed and another wounded, the last army casualties at the Bears Paw Mountains. Late that afternoon, Miles's supply wagons caught up, along with the Napoleon gun and its explosive shells. At last, the wounded could be housed in tents, which had to be moved farther away from the Nez Perce sharpshooters, who fired at their lighted glow after dark. Nightfall brought chilling rain that turned to snow around midnight, and the soldiers without tents slept in wet blankets.

On the morning of October 2, messengers went back and forth between the lines, arranging a new truce. Finally Miles, Joseph, and Lieutenant Maus walked out with a white flag, and three Nez Perces brought Jerome forward. After Miles's duplicity the day before, everyone was on the alert for a new trick, or one in retaliation. But the two groups met, Joseph and Jerome shook hands, and they crossed to their own sides.

Jerome told Miles what he had seen and heard: wounded lying everywhere, the interconnected shelter pits, the continuing hope for relief by the Sioux. He had been able to count 250 people, one hundred of them warriors.

Miles tried to restart negotiations on the wintry morning of October 3, but the Nez Perce leaders were not interested. Around noon, he decided it was time to begin shelling with the Napoleon gun's fused shells, which had a range of a quarter mile. Only twenty-four shells had been transported, so he had them fired at lengthy intervals that day and throughout the day and night of October 4. The gun was aimed at the coulee filled with shelter pits, and the first shell killed a twelve-year-old girl and a grandmother and buried three women and a boy when their pit caved in. The latter four were dug free, and the others were left where they lay.

Yellow Wolf compared the soldiers' intentional shooting of noncombatants to the white men's furor over the Nez Perces' having killed the women and children in Idaho. He said, "It was bad that cannon guns should be turned on the shelter pits where [there] were no fighters. Only women and children, old and wounded men in those pits." He knew that Jerome had described the position of the pits: "Of course his business was to carry back all news he could spy out in our camp" (McWhorter, *Yellow Wolf*, p. 218).

Private Zimmer, in a battalion supporting the artillery, wrote in his journal what he heard that day of October 3:

> *Firing has been going on all day & their camp got a good shelling. But they are well fixed & intend to wear us out. Their rifle pits have underground connections, & if a shot strikes in one they crawl through to another. (Zimmer, p. 127)*

The Nez Perces ignored Colonel Miles's renewed attempts on October 4 to hold a talk. Shelling and sharpshooting continued sporadically. The temperature warmed up a bit, and the soldiers were able to go out and gather some firewood. Around dusk, General Oliver O. Howard arrived with a small group of men. Nez Perce bullets whizzed by them, making Howard at first think that Miles's pickets were mistakenly firing at their fellow soldiers. Besides twenty-three soldiers, Howard's group included interpreter Arthur Chapman, who was Joseph's former friend from Idaho, and two older Nez Perce men whose married daughters were in the besieged camp. Known to whites as Captain John and Old George, their Nez Perce names were Jokais and Meopkowit.

Howard immediately put the ambitious Miles's mind at ease when he said he had not come to take command. He would let Miles accept the surrender, which he thought would be soon. Howard hoped to help in the negotiations, but had no idea that when the Nez Perces learned of his presence they would be both dismayed and angry. Even after Miles's dirty trick in capturing Joseph under the truce flag, the Nez Perces trusted him more than they did the hated General Howard.

At eight o'clock on the sunny and much warmer morning of October 5, Miles ordered his men to stop firing. An hour later, Jokais and Meopkowit walked over to the Nez Perce camp under a white flag. While some men threatened to kill them for traveling with the white men, others waited to hear their message. Yellow Wolf heard Meopkowit urge peace negotiations. He said:

> General Miles and Chief Joseph will make friends and not let each other go today. General Miles is honest-looking man. I have been with General Howard. I was afraid myself....[but] I heard General Howard telling, "When I catch Chief Joseph, I will bring him back to his own home."
> Do not be afraid! General Miles said, "Tell Joseph we do not have any more war!" (McWhorter, Yellow Wolf, pp. 222–223)

Sending the two men back to Miles's camp, the Nez Perce leaders argued in council. Espowyes, one of the warrior chiefs, wanted reparations for farmland and livestock lost in Idaho before the war started. Others urged Joseph not to surrender because they were sure Howard would have him hanged. Repeatedly, Yellow Wolf later reported, the talk hinged on their mistrust of army intentions: "All feared to trust General Howard and his soldiers" (McWhorter, Yellow Wolf, p. 223).

Then Howard stood in plain sight and shouted across, wanting to know why the Nez Perces were not coming to negotiate. Yellow Wolf recalled that all the Nez Perces said, "General Howard does not look good. He is mean acting!" (McWhorter, Yellow Wolf, p. 223).

Jokais and Meopkowit returned to the Nez Perce camp with a message from Colonel Miles, asking to meet with Joseph. They said:

> Those generals said tell you: "We will have no more fighting. Your chiefs and some of your warriors are not seeing the truth. We sent...all our messengers to say to [you] 'we will have no more war!'" (McWhorter, Yellow Wolf, p. 224)

Joseph was relieved that, as he said,

*General [sic] Miles said, "Let's quit."*
*And now General Howard says, "Let's quit."*
*You see, it is true enough! I did not say "Let's quit!"*
*When the warriors heard those words from Chief Joseph, they answered,*
*"Yes, we believe you now." (McWhorter,* Yellow Wolf, *p. 224)*

## The War Ends

General Howard and Colonel Miles, unaware of Sherman's vindictive plans for the Nez Perces, told the people in good faith that they would be returned to the Lapwai reservation in their home country. They sent the message that, when Sturgis's troops arrived, there would be no more fighting but rather the Nez Perces would be given food and warm blankets.

Joseph gave his reply to Jokais, who went back and told it to Miles and Howard through interpreter Chapman, while Lieutenant Charles E. S. Wood recorded it, "for [his] own benefit as a literary item" (Greene, *Nez Perce Summer 1877,* p. 484).

Although far removed from Joseph's actual words, what has become known as his "surrender speech" is an eloquent and poignant statement:

*Tell General Howard I know his heart. What he told me before I have in my heart. I am tired of fighting. Our chiefs are killed. Looking Glass is dead. Tu-hul-hul-sote is dead. The old men are all dead. It is the young men who say yes or no. He who led on the young men is dead. It is cold and we have no blankets. The little children are freezing to death. My people, some of them, have run away to the hills, and have no blankets, no food; no one knows where they are—perhaps freezing to death. I want to have time to look for my children and see how many of them I can find. Maybe I shall find them among the dead. Hear me, my chiefs, I am tired; my heart is sick and sad. From where the sun now stands I will fight no more forever. (Greene,* Nez Perce Summer 1877, *p. 309)*

At nearly 2:30 P.M. on October 5, Joseph met with Colonel Miles and General Howard. He started to hand his gun to Howard, who stepped aside and indicated that Miles would receive it. During the rest of the day, Nez Perce warriors emerged from their hiding places and turned over their guns. Four hundred and eighteen Nez Perces and Palouses surrendered to the army. Joseph reminded the commanders that he could speak only for his own band and that his decision did not bind other leaders and their bands. In fact, that same night of October 5, White Bird led about fifty people toward Saskatchewan and Sitting Bull, joining about one hundred who had escaped during the siege (Greene, *Nez Perce Summer 1877*, p. 313). Howard said Joseph had "treacherously" broken the treaty, showing his lack of understanding and belief that the Nez Perces were organized like the U.S. Army.

The Indians—to General Sherman, prisoners of war—were sent on to Fort Abraham Lincoln, then to Fort Leavenworth in Kansas, where they lived in tents in the malaria-infected infield of a former racetrack. More than one hundred Nez Perces died there. The survivors were moved to the Quawpaw reservation in present-day northeastern Oklahoma, which the Nez Perces called "Eeikish Pah," the hot place. Colonel Miles protested their treatment and claimed that the surrender terms had been changed without their agreement. Over the next few years, Joseph visited Washington, D.C., to request that the Nez Perces be sent back to the Northwest, and the Presbyterian church, whose missions had served the Nez Perces in Idaho, was one of the public-interest groups that became involved. When Miles was promoted to general and assigned to head the army's District of the Columbia in 1880, he still endeavored to get the Nez Perces home, but the U.S. government bureaucracy took until 1885 to complete the process. In May 1885, the surviving 268 Nez Perces boarded a train to leave Eeikish Pah.

Even then, some Nez Perces were sent to Colville Reservation in Washington, and others to Lapwai in Idaho. Joseph and Yellow Wolf were among those who never lived in their home country again.

# BIBLIOGRAPHY

Ambrose, Stephen E. *Crazy Horse and Custer: The Parallel Lives of Two American Warriors*. Garden City, NY: Doubleday, 1975; reprint 1986, New American Library.

Brown, Mark H. *The Plainsmen of the Yellowstone: A History of the Yellowstone Basin*. New York: G. P. Putnam's Sons, 1961.

Carroll, John M., ed. *I, Varnum: The Autobiographical Reminiscences of Custer's Chief of Scouts Including His Testimony at the Reno Court of Inquiry*. Glendale, CA: The Arthur H. Clark Company, 1982.

Custer, G. A. "Battling with the Sioux on the Yellowstone." *The Galaxy*, Vol. XXX, No. 1 (July 1876), pp. 91-103.

Gibson, Stan, and Jack Hayne. "Witnesses to Carnage: The 1870 Marias Massacre in Montana." http://www.dickshovel.com/

Gray, John S. *Centennial Campaign: The Sioux War of 1876*. Ft. Collins, CO: The Old Army Press, 1976.

Greene, Jerome A. *Nez Perce Summer 1877: The U.S. Army and the Nee-Me-Poo Crisis*. Foreword by Alvin M. Josephy, Jr. Helena: Montana Historical Society Press, 2001.

————. *Yellowstone Command: Colonel Nelson A. Miles and the Great Sioux War, 1876-1877*. Lincoln: University of Nebraska Press, 1991.

Haines, Francis. *The Nez Perces: Tribesmen of the Columbia Plateau*. Norman: University of Oklahoma Press, 1955.

Hoxie, Frederick E. *Encyclopedia of North American Indians*. Boston: Houghton Mifflin Co., 1996.

Lamar, Howard E, ed. *The Reader's Encyclopedia of the American West*. New York: Thomas Y. Crowell Company, 1977.

Lass, William E. "Steamboats on the Yellowstone" in Paul L. Hedren, ed. *The Great Sioux War 1877-77: The Best from* Montana: The Magazine of Western History. Helena: Montana Historical Society Press, 1991.

Laughy, Linwood, comp. *In Pursuit of the Nez Perces: The Nez Perce War of 1877*. Wrangell, Alaska: Mountain Meadows Press, 1993.

Libby, Orin Grant, ed. "The Arikara Narrative of the Campaign Against the Hostile Dakotas, 1876," *North Dakota Historical Collections*, VI, Bismarck, 1920. Quoted in Stewart, *Custer's Luck*.

McClernand, Edward J. *With the Indian and the Buffalo in Montana, 1870-1878: Including an Account of the Sioux Expedition of 1876 and the Rescue of the Remnant of Custer's Command at the Little Big Horn and with the "Journal of Marches Under Colonel John Gibbon, April 1 to September 29, 1876."* Glendale, CA: The Arthur H. Clark Company, 1969.

McDonald, Donald. "Through Nez Perce Eyes: A Trust Betrayed." In Laughy, *In Pursuit of the Nez Perces.*

McWhorter, Lucullus V. *Hear Me, My Chiefs! Nez Perce History and Legend.* Edited by Ruth Bordin. Caldwell, ID: Caxton Printers, Ltd., 1952.

————. *Yellow Wolf: His Own Story.* Caldwell, ID: The Caxton Printers, Ltd., 1940.

Moulton, Gary E. *The Definitive Journals of the Lewis & Clark: Over the Rockies to St. Louis.* Volume 8 of the Nebraska Edition. Lincoln: University of Nebraska Press, 2002.

Nez Perce National Historic Trail. http://www.fs.fed.us/npnht/autotours/

Pearson, Jeffrey V. "Nelson A. Miles, Crazy Horse, and the Battle of Wolf Mountains." *Montana: The Magazine of Western History,* 51 (Winter 2001), 53-67.

Richards, Raymond, "The Human Interest of the Custer Battle," in *The Teepee Book: Official Publication, The Fiftieth Anniversary of the Custer Battle, 1876-1926* (n.d., National Custer Memorial Association; reprint, with additional text, of *The Teepee Book,* Vol. II, No. VI (June 1916), The Mills Company, Sheridan [WY], 1926.)

Ronda, James P. *Lewis and Clark Among the Indians.* Lincoln: University of Nebraska Press, 2002.

Ryan, John M. "Recollections," *Hardin (MT) Tribune,* June 22, 1923.

Scott, Douglas D., P. Willey, and Melissa A. Connor. *They Died with Custer: Soldiers' Bones from the Battle of the Little Bighorn.* Norman: University of Oklahoma Press, 1998.

Thackeray, Lorna. "Amateur Archaeologists Probe Baker Battle of 1872." *Billings (MT) Gazette,* May 7, 2000. http://www.billingsgazette.com/

Tolman, Newton F. *The Search for General Miles.* New York: G. P. Putnam's Sons, 1968.

Utley, Robert Marshall. *The Lance and the Shield: The Life and Times of Sitting Bull.* New York: Henry Holt & Company, Inc., 1993; reprint 1994, Ballantine Books.

Vaughn, J. W. *The Reynolds Campaign on Powder River.* Norman: University of Oklahoma Press, 1961.

————. *With Crook at the Rosebud.* Harrisburg, PA: The Stackpole Co., 1956.

Viola, Herman J. *It Is a Good Day To Die: Indian Eyewitnesses Tell the Story of the Battle of the Little Bighorn.* New York: Crown Publishers, Inc., 1998.

Welch, James, with Paul Stekler. *Killing Custer: The Battle of the Little Bighorn and the Fate of the Plains Indians.* New York: W. W. Norton & Co., 1994.

Young, Steve. "A Broken Treaty Haunts the Black Hills." *Argus Leader* [Sioux Falls, SD]. June 27, 2001. http://www.argusleader.com/

Zimmer, Private William F. *Frontier Soldier: An Enlisted Man's Journal of the Sioux and Nez Perce Campaigns, 1877.* Edited and annotated by Jerome A. Greene. Helena: Montana Historical Society Press, 1998.

# INDEX

**219**

*About the Author*

Barbara Fifer writes and edits from Helena, Montana,
and is the author of ten books of popular history and geography.